The Work of This Moment

THE WORK OF
THIS MOMENT

Toni Packer

Charles E. Tuttle Co., Inc.
Boston • Rutland, Vermont • Tokyo

Published in 1995 by Charles E. Tuttle Company, Inc. of Rutland, Vermont and Tokyo, Japan, with editorial offices at 153 Milk Street, Boston, Massachusetts, 02109

Portions of this book appeared in *The Work of This Moment: Awareness in Daily Life*, privately published by Springwater Center in 1988. The book was first published in its entirety by Shambhala Publications in 1990.

Library of Congress Cataloging-in Publication Data

Packer, Toni, 1927–
    The work of this moment / Toni Packer. —1st ed.
      p. cm.
    ISBN 0-8048-3062-2
1. Spiritual life. 2. Spiritual life (Zen Buddhism) I. Title.
BL624.P23 1990
294.3'4448—dc20   89–43312
                                         CIP

Cover photography © 1995 Marjorie Nichols
Cover design by Sherry Fatla

3 5 7 9 10 8 6 4

Printed in the United States of America

*The emergence and blossoming of understanding,
love, and intelligence has nothing to do with any
tradition, no matter how ancient or impressive—it
has nothing to do with time. It happens on its own
when a human being questions, wonders, inquires,
listens, and looks silently without getting stuck in
fear, pleasure, and pain. When self-concern is
quiet, in abeyance, heaven and earth are open.
The mystery, the essence of all life, is not separate
from the silent openness of simple listening.*

—TONI PACKER

Contents

Acknowledgments

My heartfelt thanks to everyone who has helped with this book: to Lenore Friedman for writing the introduction; to all the friends who let us use their letters; to Peter Turner of Shambhala Publications for his care and understanding in reading, arranging, and editing; to past and present members of the Springwater Center staff whose help on the earlier, self-published work contributed greatly to the present volume, in particular to Betsy MacLean for her work in production, to Kevin Frank for coordinating its early stages, to Sally Fox, Stewart Glick, Deborah Kirsten-Hass, Susan McCallum, and Doris Weber for transcribing, typing, and proofreading, to Sally Woodmansee and Matt Haas for their many valuable suggestions; to my husband, Kyle, for being there for whatever was needed; and to everyone interested in questioning and listening to the unfathomableness of this moment.

Introduction by LENORE FRIEDMAN

It's not a simple matter to talk about Toni Packer. It's not a matter of simply saying she's this, or that, *not* this, *not* that. (I imagine her sitting just behind my left shoulder, smiling, eyes lifted questioningly, humorously, at whatever I say.) When I first met her in 1983, she was a Zen teacher, though she no longer considered herself a Buddhist. Today she is not a Zen teacher. (Or is she? Some feel she teaches the essence of Zen.) In fact she says she's not a teacher at all. (What is she *doing*, then? And why are all those people sitting and listening to what she says?) Sometimes she calls herself and "those people" coquestioners, or friends, who are inquiring into the nature of things together. "Let's look at this together," she will say, or, "Let's start from scratch together, and see where we get."

The year before I met her I'd been listening to a number of her talks on tape. From time to time I would suddenly hear the sound of "Mu . . . u . . . u . . . u!" echoing from somewhere in the background. Having studied Zen for some years by then, I knew that "Mu" was one of the first koans (teaching stories or puzzles that defy rational thinking) assigned to traditional Zen students, who would be instructed to work on it unceasingly. I'd never heard it worked on out loud, however, in full voice, abruptly punctuating a teacher's talk. Apparently this was a custom some of Toni's students carried with them directly from their Rochester Zen Center training. It was a remnant that died out quite quickly since, along with Toni, they had left behind most of the traditional features of Zen practice (bowing, chanting, incense, hierarchical structures). Such practices interfered, Toni felt, with the very thing she was most interested in: awareness—the fundamental process of looking, listening, inquiring into *everything*.

In the fall of 1983 I interviewed Toni (for my book *Meetings with Remarkable Women*) at the Genesee Valley Zen Center in Rochester, New York, which she and a number of her students had established in early 1982. By the time of my visit, the atmosphere was relatively peaceful, but two years earlier the Center had been the focus of a series of events that had split Rochester's Zen Buddhist community down the middle. The storms and shakings produced were still being absorbed, not only in Rochester but in Buddhist communities around the country.

What happened, in brief, was that Toni Packer, then chosen successor to Philip Kapleau (venerable *roshi* of Rochester Zen Center), after painful and patient self-questioning, severed her ties with traditional Buddhism and began teaching what she then called "Zen work" in a fresh, unbeholden way. Since that time there have been other dramatic events in other Zen communities in our country. But this one was perhaps the most seminal, most prophetic. Without implying a simple cause and effect, one senses a connection between what happened in Rochester and the fact that, in other centers across the country, the radical question of what Zen should look and feel like in America today is being openly asked and pondered out loud.

At the time of my visit I had heard sketchily of the events in Rochester and, after listening to Toni's powerful, resonant voice on tape, I had formed the impression of a brilliant mind and a commanding personality. I was looking forward to meeting her with anticipation, and not a little awe.

It was already dark and the ground and hedges were wet with recent rain, the evening I arrived at GVZC. There were no lights in the windows of the big stone house, and no one answered my knock after I hauled my valise up the front steps. Then I noticed a sign directing me around to the side door. Halfway there, I saw two people walking up the drive. The tall one, a young man, introduced himself. "And this is Toni," he said. I automatically said, "Hi, Toni," and then stopped. "You mean *Toni*-Toni?"

We all laughed. I had been taken aback because Toni of the powerful voice was just a person: in a knitted cap and goose-down jacket, face pink from outdoors, smile welcoming me, eyes blue and very bright, short silver hair just showing under the cap.

Just a person. I recognized the voice, but the kindness in it now touched me. I was tired and my head was aching. In the kitchen we sat down at a long wooden table in the middle of the warm, spacious room, and soon someone was making tea.

As my body relaxed, I became aware of Toni's presence across the table. She sat there very quietly, very simply. No need for words. Just stillness, and non-intrusive being there. Over the next few days, and in subsequent encounters elsewhere, I learned that Toni brings these qualities with her, into whatever room or situation.

The next day Toni and I sat in her bright, pleasant upstairs room for our first extended talk. I learned that she was born in Berlin in 1927, her childhood darkened by the horrors of Hitler and Nazism. She was only six years old when Hitler came to power. Since her mother was Jewish, there was considerable fear within the family, and in order to protect the children, Toni and her older sister and her stepbrother were baptized. Toni remembers the Lutheran minister coming to the house and sprinkling water on them. She also remembers the real religious fervor that came up later, a yearning for something beyond herself. She was haunted by questions about the war and the persecution of the Jews. Her parents were very careful, afraid to speak freely in front of the children lest they repeat something outside that could be dangerous to them. Friends and schoolmates were wearing the uniform of the youth movement. Toni envied them, would have felt more secure wearing the tie and leather knot, though what it all meant was unclear. Then came the bombing, the nightmare of terror and destruction. How, Toni wondered, could this be compatible with the notion of a loving God who looked after his children and protected them? It made no sense to her.

She was also troubled by a feeling of guilt that never left her. If Jesus died on the cross to take on himself the sins of the world, why did she still feel guilty? Why hadn't he taken away her guilt? Gathering her courage one day, she asked the minister about these things. But with a curt remark, he withdrew. He didn't want to deal with Toni's questions at all.

Another thing she remembers is the first bombing attack. She and her sister were sick in bed with diarrhea. But when the raid began, they jumped out of bed, diarrhea gone, weakness gone. "There was tremendous energy and right action. You knew just what you needed to do." They helped put out the fires. But later, when it was all over, the thoughts flooded back in. "Oh, my God, what happened? What could have happened?" Tremendous depression set in, and then, very powerfully, the question arose: "What is the meaning of this life?" It caught her, wouldn't let go.

It was with her daily—nagging, goading. What was the meaning of this life that was so utterly nonsensical, incomprehensible, cruel? Where could she find out why we do the things we do?

Later the family moved to Switzerland, and it was there that Toni met a young American student named Kyle Packer. They were married in 1950, came to the United States the following year, and settled in upstate New York, where Kyle encouraged Toni to attend college at the University of Buffalo. In 1958 they adopted a week-old baby boy and named him Ralph. Although Toni did graduate work in psychology she found the program highly behavioristic, with much of its focus on testing, theories of learning, and experimentation with rats. Toni's interests lay elsewhere, and before very long, she left. On her own she read Freud, Jung, and Joseph Campbell, especially Campbell's four-volume *Masks of God*.

"I think that in these books I made my peace with the whole problem of the feminine—partly by seeing that it is also a cultural thing, and that there were times when female goddesses reigned high. That was before the warriors and charioteers and horseback riders came and conquered with superior power and imposed a more masculine and very often suppressive religious system. This whole problem lost its sting for me. I saw that it was a relative and conditioned thing, who was in power and who suppressed whom. There was rivalry on both sides, and fear of one another. The male fear of the feminine, and women's fear of suppression by a man. But it could shift at any time."

It was during this period that she first encountered Buddhism. And, exactly as it had been for me and many others of our generation, it was through the work of Alan Watts. She read all his books, then D. T. Suzuki's and many more. At the point of her saturation with Buddhist philosophy, Kyle brought home Philip Kapleau's *Three Pillars of Zen*. She recalls leafing through it halfheartedly, like someone presented with an extra dessert after an over-rich meal. She checked idly for references to Alan Watts, found them all quite critical, and then noticed the first instructions she'd ever seen about meditation. She sat upright. Here was something she could actually *do*.

Before long she was sitting zazen regularly at home. Then, some months later, Kapleau's book came out in paperback, and on the back cover Toni read that he had established a center in Rochester, New York. This was in 1967, when she and her family were living in North Tonawanda, a small town between Buffalo and Niagara Falls. Rochester was only an hour and a half away. She and Kyle drove there together, took a series of introductory classes, and joined the center.

Toni remembers her first impression vividly. As a child she had been accustomed to visiting German cathedrals whenever the family went touring. They had seemed impressive and mysterious, with the smell of incense and areas corded off where no one could go. What was beyond the red velvet cord? In Rochester, after an introductory lecture in the dining room, everyone was invited into the sitting room. Here, to be sure, there was incense, and a Buddha figure—but no cording off. You could be right there with it all. You could have an altar in your own home, with a Buddha figure of your own. And he was not a god, but someone like yourself, and there was a practice and a discipline open to anyone, without distinction. No boundaries.

Very soon Toni was attending *sesshins* (meditation retreats) and working on koans with Kapleau-roshi. Their relationship grew in mutual respect and affection. In a very early *dokusan* (a private meeting between teacher and student) he told her that if she ever taught, she would not have to teach the way he did. She was startled. At the time the thought of teaching was furthest from her mind, but she remembered what he said. Years later his words took on greater meaning, and he never withdrew them, though the consequences caused him pain. There was special poignance in the situation because not long before he said these words to Toni, Kapleau-roshi had himself broken with his own revered Japanese master, Yasutani-roshi. Yasutani had irrevocably opposed changes that Kapleau felt were necessary in transplanting Zen to this new country.

For Toni, finding Zen practice was like finding food she had been hungry for without quite knowing it. She plunged in with her whole mind and body. She worked hard, with freshness and intensity, finding energy to spare. Her intelligence was challenged as never before. Her deepest questions could be held and plumbed until only questioning remained. For a long time the forms did not oppress her. They provided a structure to work within.

Most Buddhist scriptures, however, she found too elaborate, dry, inaccessible. Could she experience what they were talking about for herself? That was the only thing that made sense to her. Finally, in a book by W. Y. Evans-Wentz called *Tibetan Yoga and Secret Doctrines,* she found a few passages that spoke to her directly. They concerned a number of practices for relating to thoughts during meditation, such as cutting them off, following a thought to its end, or letting thoughts roam freely. Then the practitioner is likened to someone sitting on the bank of a stream, letting thoughts just stream by. But even here, thought processes are still being employed; one is still thinking. One is using thought to detect thought. Seeing this is the first step.

"I can't tell you how often I read this," Toni told me, "and what joy there was in understanding something—not verbally, but the words leading you to understanding something directly. Being able to see directly how this mind works. So that one is not trapped by it, doesn't deceive oneself, and doesn't deceive others. Which happens easily enough. Without attention or awareness, that's what happens!"

In the early 1970s she was being asked to counsel students about personal concerns or psychological problems coming up in practice, and then to give public talks on Zen at universities and other places. Each step of the way she felt pushed a bit beyond herself. More a private than a public person, she would not have sought these activities. But it had been part of her training that when your teacher asked you to do something, you said yes. So when Roshi asked, she complied.

At the same time, her perspective began to widen. With her contacts outside the center, with new students, and with old students whose concerns she was listening to, she was no longer focused only on her own work. She began to perceive some of the traditional forms in a new way. Bowing, for instance.

She had learned that bowing can come from a place of selflessness. Prostrating before the altar or before Roshi in dokusan could happen out of emptiness. But now, when students came to her and bowed to her, were they seeing her clearly or putting her above them as an image? And could she be sure that she was not feeling herself thus raised up? What images were being created in both their minds? Even though she was wary of—aware of—these things, students might not be.

And what of chanting? There were many chants, and they were long, and often were repeated rapidly several times in succession. What was the purpose of this? If the meaning was important, wouldn't speaking the words more slowly avoid the pitfall of speaking them mechanically, by rote?

Toni was also seriously questioning the harsh and often merciless use of the *kyosaku* (hitting stick), with which meditating students were whacked on the shoulders to arouse their energies. She was deeply concerned about what the hitting was doing to the minds and bodies of the people being hit. Likewise, what was it doing to those who were wielding the stick? The use of the stick was reverentially referred to as an act of compassion. But did stick wielding really arise from compassion? And didn't energy awaken naturally in the course of questioning? (Later on, at her new center, the practice of using the stick would be abandoned altogether.)

Toni's mind could allow such questions to arise and be looked at. She did not need to react or to act in any way. She paid attention. She considered. She took her time. She could not carry out practices that felt wrong to her. She consulted with a few friends. And gradually she began to make a small formal change here and there.

This was at a time when she and Roshi were teaching in tandem. He would be gone for months at a time, vacationing as well as traveling to other centers in this country and abroad, and Toni had been asked to take charge in his absence. As early as 1975, he had called Toni into his office and told her that he was thinking about retirement, possibly in five years. He would probably move to a warmer climate with a small number of disciples. And he wanted her to take over the Rochester center entirely when this happened. Would she be willing?

Toni was thunderstruck. She remembers driving home with a sinking heart to tell Kyle. Though it would not take place for several years, the prospect lay on her heavily, like a stone. She didn't know how to take such a responsibility. She couldn't continue doing things the way they were being done; she knew that clearly by this time. But was she capable of doing them differently?

Still, she told Roshi yes. Her training left her no alternative.

It was sometime in the mid-seventies, in a book that Roshi himself had loaned her (Jacob Needleman's *The New Religions*), that she came across the teachings of Krishnamurti for the first time. The effect was catalytic. The way Toni puts it, "Veils started dropping from my eyes." All her questions were stretched further. In Krishnamurti's words was the clear and simple expression of truth without the use of any religious trappings whatsoever. It became inescapably clear to her that while the Zen tradition claimed an absence of symbols, dogma, rituals, and creeds, at the very same time an elaborate system of ceremonies, etiquette, beliefs, transmission of teachings, and devotional activities was an important, often compulsory, and amazingly unquestioned aspect of the actual training.

Now, a radically new way of working opened up as she carefully read all the books by Krishnamurti that she could get her hands on. Together with Kyle, she also attended many of his talks in California, Switzerland, and England. And over the course of several years, there gradually unfolded for her a way of combining quiet sitting with direct, intensive questioning, a way of looking into fundamental human problems within oneself, in the context of silent retreats, talks, and individual meetings with students.

Krishnamurti says: Shun all systems, all authority, all images. End your particular attachment, now. The mind must be free of all authorities. And, as if echoing the Buddha's last words to his disciples: Be a light to yourself. Krishnamurti also said, in a discourse on love, "It may mean complete upheaval; it may break up the family . . . you may have to shatter the house you have built; you may never go back to the temple." Whether or not Toni read those particular words, they speak uncannily of the upheaval that was to follow.

At the beginning of 1981, Kapleau-roshi left for a year's sabbatical and Toni was put in charge of the center. She was still trying at this time to find a way to be true to her own inner perception and at the same time remain loyal to her teacher and the tradition precious to him. She wrote down all the things she felt needed changing, like the wording of certain vows and sutras, the pace of chanting, and she dropped special seating and etiquette that denoted hierarchy, as well as the compulsory sitting requirement for staff—all sittings became voluntary. When she spoke to Roshi about these things, he was disconcerted. Why did she want to go so fast? He acceded to the slower chanting, but wanted her to leave other things the way they were. Under Harada-roshi (one of his own masters), he said, a new teacher would not have dreamed of changing anything. That would have been outright impudence. What you do in dokusan, he said to her, is up to you. But the forms were another matter. "We've created something here."

Toni realized how strongly he felt that it was *his* center, and how much he didn't want it changed—at least not so quickly. And to the latter, at that point, she agreed.

She wanted it to work. She struggled to make it work, to find an accommodation that would harmonize this conflict. According to some of her students, they were themselves in favor of her leaving the situation long before she was. They described acute division at the center at the time, turbulent meetings during which Toni's actions were criticized. And all the while Toni knew they were seeing only the ripples of a much deeper shift within her.

"I began to question this whole thing I was doing," she told me. "Belonging to a group, and the identification with it. But I tried to rationalize it away. I didn't want to tackle it. I was part and parcel of it."

Problems were bound to arise. For example, there was the incident of the *rakusu*. At Rochester Zen Center, the rakusu (a loose, elaborately constructed vest worn over one's robes or ordinary clothing) was awarded to those students who had passed their initial koans, and carried with it inescapable elements of prestige and attainment. Toni took hers off and never put it on again.

She must have known this would not go unnoticed. Yet this and the other changes that she had already instituted were actually far behind the current reaches of her mind. So the depth of some people's opposition shocked and disheartened her. If there had been any other path, she would have taken it. Conflict and confrontation were painful and exhausting to her, raising specters from her childhood. But she could not go backward, or sideways either. To see through delusion, you cannot promote delusion.

Rakusus, prostrations, special seats in the zendo—all meant separation. However many times she looked at it, she had to go forward.

A significant meeting took place when Kapleau-roshi returned to Rochester from Santa Fe in June 1981. People had been writing and talking to him, complaining about the changes that had been taking place. In a roomful of indignant people, Toni was permitted to have only two staff members with her. Accusations were leveled at all three. By the end of the meeting, and even after the earnest intervention of a long-time member in a discussion that lasted until two-thirty in the morning, she knew that ultimately, if not immediately, she would have to leave—despite the heartache it would cause, despite the division. There were couples, for example, one of whom was her student and the other Roshi's. How would they negotiate separate allegiances? These questions would have to be faced. It would be painful. It would take time. But first the separation would have to take place.

Toni was aware that the whole situation had also been sapping her health. "Some people would love this type of thing, thrive on it. Whereas for me, having grown up in Hitler's Germany, this really touched off a lot of old fears—of being accused, of being denounced."

And the much deeper issue—was she still a Buddhist?—had not even been raised yet. She knew that sooner or later she would have to raise it, but she hadn't yet faced it completely. She still could not just abandon the whole thing. So when Roshi said the day after the meeting, "If you stay, you can do anything you want. I give you complete freedom to work in your own way," she agreed to stay. But in relating the events to me later, she said: "Before long I knew he couldn't give me that 'complete' freedom, because I wasn't going to carry on with Buddhism anymore."

"How did that become clear?" I asked.

"Well, I myself was doing all these prostrations, and lighting incense, and bowing, and the whole thing. I realized that I was influencing people, just by the position I was in, the whole setup. I could see it, and I wasn't going to have any part in it anymore.

"Unless you are really set on discovering, if anybody supports you in *not* discovering, you won't do it. Which I found in Zen. The system is very supportive to *not* questioning some things. Even though it claims to question everything. You question everything and you 'burn the Buddha,' but then you put him back up!

"I examined very carefully: Did I have any division while I was bowing? It had always been said, 'When you bow, you're not bowing to the Buddha, you're bowing to yourself. And when you're prostrating, everything disappears, you disappear, the Buddha disappears and there's nothing.' I looked carefully and it wasn't completely clear. I could see there was often an image of the bower, or of the person who 'has nothing.' Often there was a shadow of something, somebody there who was doing it. Or maybe the idea of being able to do it emptily!"

"Let me ask you something. Is it OK to bow if you're empty?"

"Why do you do it? Why do I do it? Let me ask you this: If you had never come in touch with this particular tradition of bowing, in a moment of deep understanding or profound outpouring of love—would you bow?"

"Well, in a way I've learned to. I've learned this gesture as an expression of respect and gratitude and love. And sometimes it just comes spontaneously to me."

"Do you then teach others to do that? People in the West, who haven't been taught to do this, don't do so spontaneously."

"You might convey an empty gesture?"

"Yes. Love you cannot teach. It's either in you or it's not, and how it expresses itself, or whether it expresses itself at all in gestures, is irrelevant."

In the end, the pieces began to come together with a kind of inevitability. And despite some of her students' experience of a lengthy process, it all seems to have happened remarkably quickly. Toni had been left in charge of the center on January 1, 1981, when Kapleau-roshi moved to Santa Fe. In June he returned to Rochester for the stormy meeting described above. In November Toni went to visit him in Mexico, where he was vacationing, to tell him she could not go on because she no longer considered herself a Buddhist. "It was very difficult for me to do. If he had wanted me to stay another year, then I would have stayed, even within the old framework." But after talking to the trustees, he only asked her to stay till January. So the whole story took place in one year's time.

From another vantage point, however, it went on much longer. Wounds healed slowly. There was criticism, bitterness, a sense of loss. While many students joined one center or the other, some remained unaffiliated, wary, even disillusioned. Some deeply wanted to work toward healing the schism. The very phenomenon of two Zen centers in one city felt discordant, antithetical to notions of harmony and nondivision. Some examined their own behavior and ways of thinking that contributed to polarization. One student wrote Toni a letter, which she quoted in a Sunday talk, deploring the ways in which "we too have kept alive the division between the two sanghas."

In characteristic fashion Toni said, "There are not two sanghas. There are only human beings, split and divided within themselves." She was not impatient for peace and harmony. Rather, she wanted to know: What are peace and harmony? Whether we're talking about two nations, two centers, two individuals, or the inner state of one individual, what we're dealing with are thoughts, ideas, imagination. "Do you see that?" She knew that many found this disconcerting, would fight it with all their being. But as a child in Germany, Toni had experienced the travesty of periods of "peace" that were only intervals between wars.

All of us are moved to solve problems in the world, she says, yet we're not in touch with the problem directly. We bring our confusion to the situation. We may have some limited, temporary impact, but not the real answer. For that we would need to enter into the problem and see it fundamentally, in ourselves.

How can we contribute to peace and harmony when there is no peace and harmony in ourselves? And genuine peacefulness and harmony must be differentiated from some idea that one repeats, some "image of oneself as someone who works for peace and harmony." Such images prevent our seeing the disharmony in ourselves, the division, the fragmentation.

So Toni was not in a hurry to cover over whatever raw feelings there were, even in the service of peacefulness or love. Division was real. Anger and bitterness and self-interest were real. Why cover them over before looking at them, experiencing them, understanding how they arise?

"What is the source of hatred, violence, war, dissension, division? If one is consumed with this problem—it is destroying the world—where does one start?"

Toni starts with the self. Because as long as there is self-interest, it will collide with another self-interest. And until we come together as one, there will be no peace.

Again and again she emphasizes the importance of nondefensive listening. And her ability to remain open and friendly toward criticism of every kind can be very disarming. She has based a number of talks on pointed and challenging questions from some of her students. (One asked: "Isn't what you're doing just psychology? What about enlightenment, or becoming a buddha?" Another wrote: "My only fear is for those of your students who are too blinded by your eloquence and beauty of personality to find their own true path.") She inaugurated a series of discussion periods to address any and all questions that might arise in relation to the changes at the new center. These discussions are ongoing.

We need to listen to each other, and to ourselves, without any threat, she says. And this can happen only if there really is no threat—which is no easy matter at all. It takes "tremendous attention, and energy of awareness, not to be pulled into all these tendencies blindly." It is so easy not to look at what is happening in ourselves when we are defensive, ambitious, envious, or disparaging of others. Where do these reactions come from? What is the source of disharmony, war, the lack of relationship among human beings? We must look and ask and sit with these questions. Again and again: What is it?

What, even, is Buddhism? Who knows? she asks. Who can really know? She recalls again the Buddha's words: Be a lamp unto yourself. Rely on the truth and take refuge in nothing else.

That is what Toni teaches, whether or not she calls herself a Buddhist. She teaches—she is—this questioning lamp, casting light on whatever arises or comes her way. "It's possible for a human being to see, not just think about it. But you have to sit and let the question sit, and just look and listen internally, without knowing."

Toni teaches by questioning. She questions not only all your beliefs and conditioning, but also the usual framework of teacher and student. She is not there to give you anything, nor to impart the truth. There is something taking place; but it has nothing to do with a giver and a receiver. Two minds are meeting and, if there is openness, something may move, shift, clarify. "Do you see that?" Toni will say, again and again. Or, "Can there just be listening, without wanting, without preferring this to that?"

Her words are never meant to persuade or convince or even to inspire. Words are not the truth. Truth is direct seeing, and it cannot be taught. "In clear seeing there is neither 'teacher' nor 'student'. There is no division." There are two people, whose minds are much more alike than not, raising questions together, looking at "the whole thing" together, attending, attending, again and again. Sometimes clarification happens. Sometimes not.

In May 1983, on the eve of GVZC's first annual meeting as an organization, Toni talked about "who and what we are—and what we're not." She said that this organization is important only insofar as it helps each person see into and understand himself or herself without delusion. She emphasized the danger that an organization could become more important than the people it was created to serve. That it could become an object of pride and attachment. That it could promote arrogance and division from others. "What is a center?" she asked. Does it create images of self-importance, status, prestige? These things need to be clarified, continually, "so nothing grows unawares."

She talked about how ideals can blind us to what actually takes place in our hearts, minds, and bodies. We repress and deny our shortcomings, then see them clearly in others. How sensitive relationships are between human beings, she said. They require so much love—and so often it is inadequate. She recalled the first time she confronted her mother with the fact that she had been afraid of her most of her life. Her mother wouldn't hear it, couldn't believe it.

"It was such a revelation. I thought she knew it, but she didn't. And she hadn't meant to be that way. She had this 'ideal' of being good and loving! So ideals are worthless, dangerous, blinding, hindering. And we constantly build them up and take our refuge in them."

No organizational form, she said, however rationally conceived, can ensure against dangers. It cannot be aware. It's only a set of words, a concept. "We have to do the work. If there's not this love, this attention to other people and oneself, how can the rules take care of it?" Each person must become aware of impulses toward domination over others, for example, or for the security that comes from blind obedience.

"This center was not formed to enshrine a creed, or the creed of no-creed. Not the idea of anything nor the idea of nothing. When there is nothing, there is no need for any belief. *Nothing* cannot be symbolized. It's the absence of self-centeredness and fear for oneself. Who am I when I have nothing to represent me?"

She went on, that evening, to say some very interesting things about "enclosures." There is so much in all of us that is unexplored. And it is so deep, so dark. The fear of not-being, for example, the fear of evil, of destructiveness and violence. And there is such a longing for something beyond all these, something beyond the triteness of the everyday, beyond the endless difficulties of relationship. And it seems as if, since time immemorial, enclosures have been especially conducive to what assuages these fears: to projection, propitiation, worship, magic, ceremony. She cited the Cro-Magnon caves at Lascaux, the "temple caves," they have been called, and the Gothic cathedrals of Europe "where everything is drawn upward—the architecture does it for you. You shiver all over." And forget to ask: Where does this come from? Who built this? Who painted the icons? Who wrote the scriptures? And who interprets them?

So one must be very cautious when one builds an enclosure. One must observe what happens within it. Within *this* enclosure too, she added, referring to the enclosure of the self. Until one starts questioning—what is this self?—it is not clear that it is an enclosure, that it separates us from others, from nature. One sees and touches and contacts the world through one's past experiences, and these color everything, determine one's whole approach. "I see everything through my tinted glasses. Is it possible to take them off?"

Without walls, she said, there are no enclosures. There is space. There is no inside or outside. If we cling to an organization, if we're attached or dependent on it, isn't this like the enclosure of the self? Are we seeking protection in the wider enclosure of a center? "To explore this we must step outside, not run away into something else again. Is it possible?"

Toni constantly engages her hearers in this fashion. All her talks approach dialogue. Her questions echo in the mind, setting off responses and questions of one's own. Later in this talk she referred to a poem in the *Mumonkan* ("The Gateless Gate") that contains the line: *You must climb a mountain of swords with bare feet.* "So can one walk with great care, aware of dangers, not panicky, but stepping carefully? Relating with care, listening with care, really with care, to oneself and the person right next to you?"

In the journal I kept of my Rochester trip, the first entry reads: "She is like clear, sparkling water. Her eyes see the truth and there she is. Just there. She is utterly, simply kind. No wanting, no expectation."

A later entry reads: "I have no difficulty imagining her holding that fundamental question always. That is how I experience her: in the middle of 'what is it?'—always. So nothing else confuses or interferes. Nothing else unbalances. It's not even that the question goes on behind anything else in the foreground. Everything else is permeated by the question, organized by it, illuminated by it.

"And I suppose that would affect the self, the personality. Of course—the question does not come from the personality, since even that (especially that?) is being questioned."

Reading this over now, I see how many "ideas" it holds. And how these separate me from Toni, separate me from my own experience. Yet they communicate something, if not truth, and therefore I leave them—especially the clear, sparkling water.

In the years since my visit to the Genesee Valley Zen Center in 1983, a number of significant changes have occurred. The first was the purchase in early 1984 of 284 acres of undeveloped land for a new retreat center in Springwater, New York, an hour's drive south of Rochester. Roads had to be built and housing construction started from scratch, but by the spring of 1985, though much work remained to be done, Toni held her first country retreat there. Soon, the major activity of GVZC gradually shifted to the Springwater site, although a smaller Rochester center has continued to be maintained as well.

In 1986, a radical change in the center's name was decided upon. For some time Toni had been concerned that the term *Zen* evoked images that were not consonant with the actual work she and those working with her were doing. In a letter to members she wrote: "Although the word *Zen* can be used in a universal sense, to most people it refers to a separate religious tradition. It is associated in people's minds not only with Buddhism, but also with Japanese traditions. Its use is linked with specific training methods and goals, and brings with it the image of the *"Zen"* person. Being linked with a specific tradition results in compartmentalization, division, and isolation. It would be good to use a name that is simple and direct."

A number of new names were considered, most retaining the name Genesee Valley. In the end the choice went beyond them to Springwater Center, the simplest and most direct of all.

Another important development, especially for people living on the West Coast, has been Toni's now annual trip to California. She came for the first time in May 1985, to conduct a five-day retreat at Olema, an hour's drive up the coast from San Francisco. There were twenty-six of us, sixteen women and ten men, from a wide variety of backgrounds, though many had done Zen practice for years. Only a few had met Toni in person before. The setting was beautiful: a Vedanta retreat center on two thousand acres of virgin, green, lovingly tended hillsides and woods.

The room we used for meditation happened to contain a raised dais with flowers, candles, incense, and three large portraits on the wall above it: Christ, Ramakrishna, and the Buddha. Not the most propitious setting for Toni's teaching, one might have thought. However, in almost no time, all the particulars faded, edges softened, opinions dropped away, and we sat together simply, with beginner's mind, and heard the birds singing. The birds! All day long they sang, layer upon layer into the distance. They woke during our first sitting in the morning, and if we walked outside during the first walking period, we could hear their morning calls as the sun rose. There were deer and jackrabbits too, cows that snored, and even a badger.

The whole retreat had a quality of gentleness. For some people the fact that sittings were optional was in itself revolutionary. To question everything, even the attitudinal basis behind one's practice (for instance, stoicism toward pain or exhaustion), was by turns exhilarating, scary, resistance-producing, freeing. As each response in turn was met with attentive, open curiosity, all the activities of the day, all our interactions with each other and the environment and ourselves, were experienced freshly, tenderly. On an almost molecular level, we learned about nonviolence.

Nothing was mandatory (one could bow or not bow, sit facing each other or the wall); the atmosphere was totally respectful of individual needs and rhythms. We felt encouraged to be self-reliant and to question our own motivations for practice, rather than blindly to obey even internalized authority. During morning and afternoon breaks we took long walks in the surrounding woods, followed deer trails over the hills. This unhurried, meditative time close to trees and grass and wind and creatures opened out and deepened the whole experience.

In her talks, Toni spoke about attention, about self, about death. On the last day she read long selections from Huang-po and Krishnamurti. Often she would stop, listen, and mimic the sounds of the birds outside ("whoo, whoo . . . fshsh, fshsh, fshsh"). The talks, though spontaneous, were lucid and impeccably formed. Like the rest of the retreat, the parts came together simply, naturally. Clear water flowing quietly over rocks.

In the past two years, as interest in these now week-long retreats has grown, they've been moved to a larger, though still beautiful, retreat setting in northern California. Toni is still lucid and clear, and still "just a person." The more time I spend with her the more I trust her way of working with the paradoxes of teacher or no teacher, of self or no-self, right in the jaws of the beast. I have seen her literally step aside from projections of idealized being or elevated authority. She is simply not there to receive them. New people can be startled, thrown off balance. Soon it is clear that an image in their mind is exactly that: in their mind. Old people too! We do it again and again—we still *want* somebody to put up above us, someone more perfect, more penetrating, more unbound. We abort our own perceptions. But Toni does not collude.

Her talks have become simpler. They almost always relate to specific questions posed by students (or whatever we are). So they have an intense immediacy, especially on retreat. You can *see* the unprotectedness of her posture, the vulnerability with which she talks. In individual meetings too, you are struck by her accessibility, her willingness to be with you in the very inside of yourself. Your self? . . . You look at each other in the silence.

To the Reader

The letters, articles, and dialogues contained in this book are not information to be added to our existing store of knowledge about ourselves. They are a questioning and a direct looking into the human mind manifesting in each one of us.

Is it possible as the reader to participate in this direct way? As words are being read, can the mind pause, look, and listen quietly?

In day-to-day-activities, in moment-to-moment living, can the spirit of questioning and nonjudgmental attending continue to reveal and clarify the ways of the self?

It is arduous to look at ourselves in fearless honesty, uninfluenced by ideas and images of what we are or should be. It is easier to cling to the apparent security of our automatic patterns of thinking and reacting, but these inevitably bring conflict and sorrow.

Only with clear and immediate insight can the mind begin to free itself from its conditioning, opening up to the depth of understanding that is compassion.

—TONI PACKER

The Work of This Moment

Listening and Looking

Can our relationship with each other be one of listening together and looking together? Can the images that come up be seen for what they are and be put aside so that they do not distort the listening and looking together?

At the beginning let me say something about listening and about our relationship with each other.

If one has heard talks on meditative inquiry before, what kind of listening is going on as one is hearing the talk? Is there anticipation of what is going to be said, and, as something is pointed out, is the memory-mind listening, already "knowing" what the words are all about? And what about the speaker, having given talks before? Do the words in a talk given now come out of memory mechanically, in a rote fashion?

There are different states of mind, and the state that is reacting most of the time when we are talking to each other is the state of memory. Our language comes out of memory, and we usually don't take time to think about the way we say things, let alone look carefully at what we are saying. We usually talk to each other and to ourselves in habitual, automatic ways.

So we're asking, can there be talking and listening that are not solely governed by memory and habit, except for remembrance of the language and the various examples that are given? Can there be fresh speaking and fresh listening right now, undisturbed by what is known?

When thoughts come up, "I've heard that before, I know that," can these thoughts and their effects be watched this very instant? Can there be some awareness of the narrowness and rigidity of the channel, "I know this already?" Thinking "I know this" blocks listening and seeing.

This chapter was adapted from a talk delivered on the first day of a seven-day retreat in September 1988.

Seeing is never from memory. It has no memory. It is looking now. The total organism is involved in seeing. Not thinking about what is said from memory, but listening and looking openly *now*. No one can do that for us. We can only do that ourselves, discovering directly whether what is heard, said, or read is actually so.

Most of the time we take on faith that whatever comes from a respectable or traditional source is true. But we're asking whether one can find out firsthand, not secondhand, but firsthand, first sight, whether what is said, heard, and read is actually so. Not that one takes over mechanically what someone else says. One has to be very clear within oneself that "Yes, this is so," or "No, it isn't so," or "I don't know, let me find out."

The value of a talk is to find out from moment to moment what is actually true. There's no virtue in trying to memorize what is being said, as we've been trained to do in school. Also, there is no value in attaching special importance to the person who is giving the talk. In doing that we switch from listening and looking within to thinking about the person who is talking and making that the most important thing. Creating an image of Toni and reacting to that image with reverence or rebellion, approval or disapproval, blocks immediate listening and questioning.

We do have images of each other, don't we? We can visualize someone in our mind—closing our eyes and remembering quite accurately what that person looks like. And we can verify that image by looking directly at the person. So there can be a harmless, reasonably accurate image of what someone else or oneself looks like.

But we have other than harmless, verifiable images of each other. We store up ideas about someone, about what he or she is like, based on past knowledge and experiences. We remember pleasurable experiences and painful experiences we have had with each other, and develop attachments as well as grudges based on these images. We also have ideas about each other based on ingrained prejudice, traditional lore, speculation, gossip, hearsay, wishful thinking, and so on.

These preconceived ideas and images inevitably affect our present relationship with each other. That is, memory-images deposited in the brain in the past color and distort our present perception. Each one of us can verify this. As long as I cling to the memory of the hurt you caused me or the flattering remarks you made to me, this perception of you affects our relationship right now—I will avoid you or feel drawn to you. If all of that is going on in the mind and body without being directly observed, without coming into clear awareness, I can't meet you freshly, innocently, now. Instead I'm looking at a past tape that interferes with what is coming in at this moment. Sometimes that interference is total. One is so absolutely sure about what a person is like that everything she does or says only helps to confirm the old image.

Can one observe all this intelligently because one sees and understands image creation and its effects within oneself? Oneself is the prime laboratory! Can image-building and our attachment to images be observed as they are happening in oneself so the process begins to clarify? Is it clear that the image, no matter how accurate, is not the real person? What *is* the real person?

We're asking whether one can see oneself and the other as we are this moment—not the image, not the remembrance, not the speculation or wishful thinking, not what we want to be or want that person to be for us. Not creating each other in images! We're asking very simply, "What's going on this instant, inside and out?" Can images be discovered and cease dominating, so that we can truly see ourselves and each other?

In talks, or in private meetings where we both are talking with each other, can there be a directness of communication or communion in which whatever happened in the past, yesterday, or years ago, is quite irrelevant? Can we listen and look together freshly now?

Looking and listening are not two separate processes. None of the senses are really separate. When there is no naming, no knowing, and no reacting from memory-image, the senses operate as a whole. When remembered knowledge, past experience, wanting, and fearing don't interfere, there is no sense of division as we talk with each other. There's one questioning, one listening, one looking. It's not a matter of two different people, because differences in personality are quite irrelevant. Personality develops as a result of various inherited tendencies and talents, different racial, social, and cultural programs, the ways in which we've been responded to from earliest times onward, all of our upbringing, education, and so forth. But at a moment of looking directly, now, with all the senses operating together freely, listening and feeling with an open mind, body and heart, personality doesn't matter, conditioning doesn't matter—neither is important. What is of utmost importance is the immediacy and directness of listening and seeing wholly.

What matters is not holding on to "my" opinion or "my" point of view, which is what we do. We hold on to "my way" as a very important part of our personality—I *am* my ways, my opinions and my points of view. What am I when there is no identification with them, no insisting on them, no defending them? Will one even consider such questions? Or does fear come up immediately, fear about being nothing?

This is what this work is about: facing directly the fear that arises when everything about oneself is called into question. Not called into question in order to find fault with or justify, fight or try to improve, but questioning oneself fundamentally all the way. Do you know what I mean? Where does it all come from, our identity, our deep attachment to what we are and the instantaneous defense of it? Is that all we are? What are we when there is no attachment to personality traits, to our opinions, past experiences, knowledge, and so on? Without attachment and defense, what is there? We're questioning that, not by rote, not mechanically, not purposefully, but fundamentally, with great curiosity, interest, and care.

Can our relationship with each other be one of listening together and looking together? Can the images that come up be seen for what they are and be put aside so that they do not distort the listening and looking together?

Can there be a listening that does not *abolish* the personal past— that's impossible—but that sees it for what it is: memory, thought, image, and connected feelings and emotions? That collection is not what is actual right now! When there is open listening, the past is in abeyance.

If I think that another person is able to listen better than I can, then the whole complicated mechanism of feeling inferior, inhibited, and blocked sets into motion. It comes with comparing ourselves with someone else. This is not something new now: It hooks into our collective past, comparing ourselves with others or being compared to others by teachers, parents, and friends. It brings up all the anxiety, pain, and hurt connected with past and present comparisons.

That's the amazing thing about this brain—it is associative, with all its intricate neuro-physiological connections. Something that is happening now, unless it is happening in the clarity of awareness, trails the whole past with it: feelings, emotions, reactions, and memories repressed and unrepressed. Obviously we're not islands to ourselves. We are linked to all the thoughts, feelings, and emotions that our parents and other people surrounding us had when they reacted to us—their fears, their anger, their beliefs and hopes manifest in *us*. This linkage extends to our parents' generation and their parents' generation and on and on into the infinite past including our animal ancestry. Can one observe this linkage for oneself? I can see that in reacting without awareness, habitually, automatically, the whole past is reacting, not just my personal past, but the impact of everyone and everything that I have ever been linked with. Which is everyone and everything.

Can there be a flickering of insight that what is responding right now may be the whole remembered and forgotten past? What are we actually right now—you and me? In a moment of fury I say something hurtful to you—I didn't mean to say it, I hadn't wanted to react that way, but it blurted out. Where did it come from? What was I thinking, imagining? What was I reacting to in you? Was it accurate? Did it all make sense? I don't really know! Let me look at the whole thing afresh, listen anew, inwardly and outwardly. I may be projecting something onto you or onto myself that has nothing to do with this live moment, but has everything to do with the dead past!

It seems valid to question whether there is any possibility of freedom from the past. If we look globally, leaving our own personal situation aside for the moment, we see that there has not been any diminution of fear, greed, conflict, aggression, defense, warfare, violent retaliation, and unspeakable sorrow all over the world throughout human history.

In one's immediate circle, me and you, husband, wife, companion, and children, is one constantly responding from the past, from one's own upbringing, and "raising" one's children accordingly? Do anger, fear, and violence erupt about something a child does because it's a replay of what happened in one's own life? The reaction is not deliberate, it happens automatically! One may feel right and justified, or wrong and guilty about it, but one carries on in more or less the same way. And the next generation does too, on and on.

Does one see the enormity of the problem? The burden of our whole past conditioning and its continuity? Can there be freedom from it? Not by fighting it, overcoming it, escaping from it, or drowning it out, but through direct understanding, having immediate insight into it? Insight or "seeing into" is not of the past, it is not a reaction and not a continuation of anything. It is totally fresh and uncaused, undetermined, and not dependent on anything. It happens on its own when a human being is deeply involved in wondering and questioning about oneself and one's entire relationship with others and the whole world.

Once, at a gathering in Toronto, someone said, "I'm totally confused about meditation. I've spent quite a bit of time meditating recently, several months in a retreat just this last year. There were incredible experiences during that time—marvelously blissful states. But now, finding myself in a total transition in my life, without a job and not knowing what to do to make a living, I find that these past meditation experiences don't help me at all. Not only don't they help me any, but I see that I have been using them as an escape to get away from facing my feelings of utter insecurity and fear. So what's meditation good for, what is it all about?" She didn't want to hear answers, she just needed to talk about this and question it thoroughly.

When something like this happens, when things one has been holding on to are crumbling, can one go slowly, not immediately building up something else in their stead? That's what the brain immediately tries to do: build a new structure. Rather, can one remain utterly silent with that state of uprootedness, lostness, not knowing where to go, not knowing what one really is or what it is that one has nourished and cherished, not grasping at anything? Questioning it all, holding on to nothing, open to all the fears of insecurity, pain, and sinking feelings that the physical organism produces as an accompaniment to the thoughts? Can one just be with all of that, wholly, without looking for a result? Just be with it because it's there, like the wind, the cicadas, the cool rain, the gurgling in the stomach, the breathing? That's meditation.

This feeling of uprootedness, if one really looks at it wholly, will not be named any longer. One will not know it anymore, because the knowing and the naming is the past, and this thing is *now*—it's here. Either there is escape from it or no escape. What is it when there is no escaping, no wanting it to be different? Just a new and open listening, feeling, looking, touching, tasting—all of the senses completely there. No interpretation needed.

A single thought gets the whole organism going: a sinking feeling of danger, disaster, falling apart, or whatever. One single thought can be observed to evoke all the physical symptoms of panic. This signals to the brain that there is something to be afraid of. More thoughts arise about possible dangers and escapes. What we're asking in all simplicity is: Can there be a glimpse into this whole ongoing process, not interpretation or analysis, but the immediacy of insight?

Can there be something new, something different? An instant awareness that just happens? It may, but it may immediately be overlaid by thoughts—What's going to happen to me? I don't like this, how can I get out of this?—and fantasy provides an escape. We don't lack moments of attention, what we lack is a sustained awareness of the flow of thoughts with their discomfort and anxiety. We fail to see that thoughts arise from memory of past dangers, signaling danger where there may be none. We fail to see the danger of thought itself. The content of thought is taken for reality and the immediate bodily response confirms this "reality."

Can we see this operating in an even more fundamental way? Let's look. When there are physical symptoms of fear, the thought arises that there is an entity that *has* that fear. Sensations and feelings that come up confirm that there is someone who is afraid. One talks to "oneself" about it. The fact that the origin of all this was thought and memory is lost or ignored. We believe that we are the thinker of thoughts, the doer of deeds, and further thinking will not get to the root of the problem. Can one see the limitation of thought? See directly that this thinker, this doer, is thought itself?

The mechanisms we're looking into right now are not different for you or me. North, west, east, or south, today or a thousand years ago, the same mechanisms have been operating in human beings. In discovering in oneself the mechanisms of mind and body, one is discovering the mind and body of all human beings, regardless of personality, historical time, or geographical location. That's the real beauty of this work. Because in the discovery of what is universally true for all of us, not just for me and my group, but for all of us since time immemorial, in this discovery lies the seed of compassion, of love. Love not of the personal kind, but an explosive love for everyone and everything.

Clearly, if we ask, "What is our relationship to each other?" that very expression implies a distance, a separation, doesn't it? One may put it that way, but does one see the limitation? When one really, deeply sees this, there is no distance, no separation between me and you.

Questioning

> *Real questioning has no methods, no knowing—just*
> *wondering freely, vulnerably, what it is that is*
> *actually happening inside and out. Not the word, not*
> *the idea of it, not the reaction to it, but the simple*
> *fact.*

JACEK. Toni, two years ago you attended the "Women and
American Buddhism" conference at the Providence Zen Center
and you gave a talk there on clinging to images versus clear seeing.
The talk was later published in *Primary Point*. From what I have
heard it was well received and several Dharma teachers remarked,
"She is very clear." But also some criticism emerged, like: "She has
a problem with form," "She is attached to freedom," "This is
spiritual claustrophobia"—suggesting that no matter how deep our
insight is, we always have to manifest as somebody; we need not
fear forms, but use them, and we need not fear labels imposed on
us, these come anyway. What can you say to such comments?

TONI. I don't have any problem living with "forms"—what
does it mean? We are human beings who think, feel, eat, drink,
sleep, defecate, learn, work, create, recreate, communicate with
each other, and so forth. I left an established Zen center because it
became absolutely clear that I could not continue to function and
question freely within a system dedicated to teaching and propa-
gating a specific religious tradition. It was as simple as that.

As long as there is ego investment in and identification with any
system, one cannot inquire and see clearly. Where the optic nerve
is attached to the retina, there is a blind spot where the eye cannot

---

This interview was conducted by Jacek Dobrowolski in July 1986 and
edited for publication. After the interview Jacek and Toni exchanged letters,
which have also been edited for inclusion here. Jacek, a former Zen student,
acts as translator and interpreter for Toni during her workshops and retreats
in Poland.

see. We have such blind spots wherever we are attached. Can we *see* that we are attached—become clearly aware of it? When attachment and investment are seen completely—root cause as well as the consequences that arise—then the seeing is the letting go.

The criticisms that you mentioned, as far as I can tell, come from people who may have listened to a talk by Toni (or to a talk *about* Toni), but who themselves may never have questioned deeply into the psychological conditioning that pervades every aspect of our lives. So, before speculating and expressing opinions about what Toni is doing, what her problems are and what she is attached to—if one is really interested in finding out, why not come here and question it directly with her? I am open to it whenever you come to open it up. I don't think I'll ever tire of looking at anything from scratch. The process is always newly revealing: to sit and work together to discover what is going on in the human mind and body, to question our deep-seated assumptions and conclusions, our beliefs, traditions, and teachers, and to find out why we cling in the first place.

The diagnosis "spiritual claustrophobia"—what does it mean? Does it mean being afraid of living in a "spiritual box"? Being boxed in by spiritual ideas and programs? When one actually realizes that one is trapped in a box, one steps out of it, doesn't one? The intelligence of seeing makes that possible. Claustrophobia means panicky fear of enclosure without finding a way out. The direct insight that one is caught may be the end of the confinement. If it is, one does not go back.

JACEK. I remember Soen Sa Nim's talk given last spring at the Providence Zen Center in which he said that the worst kind of mind is dictator mind; then there is no love, no equality, no freedom, and no harmony. He also mentioned that the Buddha never said: "Follow me, believe in me." Toward the end of his talk he said to his students: "You must become completely independent." Certainly you agree with such words, don't you?

TONI. It's not a matter of agreeing with anybody's words, whether they were Buddha's or anybody else's. Does one clearly understand for oneself what the person is saying, where he or she is coming from, and, if one doesn't, is one free to question it thoroughly?

Hearing the admonition "You must become completely independent," do we set up the ideal of independence? As long as we are occupied with the ideal, are we free to discover how utterly dependent we are?

When we join a spiritual group or training center, there is usually a host of activities, ceremonies, etiquettes, rituals, vows, and so forth that we are expected to participate in. There's no real freedom to choose whether to participate or not. Any hesitancy is equated with "ego," while participating in what is demanded in spite of doubts is called "lowering the mast of ego." The mind quickly becomes conditioned to the new ceremonies and to the expected ways of relating to "teachers," "senior disciples," "advanced students," and "beginners." In fact we have already been conditioned to these patterns at home, in school, at work, in church, and so forth. Now there is reinforcement of old patterns in a new place. One sees the venerated teacher participate fully and sanction what is going on. And not only this present teacher—one is ceremonially linked with a whole lineage of past teachers who have all done and sanctioned what we are doing now. So our heavy conditioning is perpetuated without any encouragement to question and doubt. On the contrary—doubting is "giving way to ego." The mind finds refuge in the whole thing. Feelings of guilt, anxiety, loneliness, and isolation are assuaged by one's belonging.

And now the teacher says: "You must become completely independent." Another teacher says: "The function of the teacher is to withhold his influence from his students." But what does that really mean? Doesn't the teacher stand for everything one has become engaged in and committed to? He or she stands for the whole past tradition! How is one going to be completely independent of that? It is an enormous question, isn't it? Can a human being be independent of the past—not in theory, but actually?

So—can one start by looking and listening to what is actually taking place from moment to moment, understanding clearly what is happening right now and what has happened in the past? How one constantly seeks refuges that one defends, rather than face fear, guilt, loneliness, insecurity?

JACEK. How one imitates . . .

TONI. How one imitates! Imitation gives a sense of belonging, a feeling of identity, and one isn't even aware of it. There is just this longing to be like someone one admires or worships—trying to be like him or her, suspending or avoiding any critical awareness.

JACEK. You have challenged the dictatorial way of teaching, but no matter how well one guards oneself against being a father or a mother figure, or any authority figure, if one speaks out with certainty, a great deal of certainty, people who hear it may try to push you into that role, or even unconsciously become dependent on you and you may not be able to detect each and every such attachment.

TONI. There are two aspects to your question. One is, does a person who speaks out with certainty, who talks to people and points out things, does that person influence the listener through personality, through the association with authority figures, through the power of words? Is the listener influenced to become a follower, an adherent who believes what is said without questioning its validity, just following or repeating mechanically what has been said?

The other question is: What happens in the person to whom many people come for help? Does this create images for her or him like, "I'm someone special, somebody important, I'm spiritually advanced, enlightened . . . ," "*I know* . . ."?

JACEK. "I know"—that's the worst one.

TONI. "I know and you *don't* know. Just do obediently whatever I tell you and eventually you may know too." Can such ideas and images be seen instantly and dispelled? One can never assume that one is beyond such images. One has to see. If they are not seen and not dispelled, they perpetuate illusion and separation.

Let's look at the first question again. All of us are vulnerable to influence by the words and actions of authority figures unless there is direct insight. If one doesn't see the truth or falsehood of what is being said, regardless of who is saying it, comprehension remains intellectual at best. Or one will just believe in the words, follow and repeat them faithfully without any insight. This kind of influence happens no matter who the speaker may be.

You also asked: Can you detect whether another person is becoming attached to you? I may or may not detect it, but we can always open up this whole question of authority and attachment in talks and meetings. We do talk about it again and again and again. Whether or not someone will really have insight into attachment and drop it . . . no one can do this for anybody else. It is up to us to discover truth for ourselves.

This brings me back to the question of what happens to the person to whom people come for help. Am I dependent upon people coming to me and listening to me? This would be a very dangerous thing. I do pay close attention to the possibility of dependence. We discuss this problem and look at it together. I think that a teacher who depends on having students inevitably uses them. How can it be otherwise? Can there be freedom and love when there is dependency and attachment of any kind? So I feel that I am utterly responsible for what I am doing and saying, but how people receive it, use it, interpret or misinterpret it is not up to me alone.

JACEK. What you say in your talks is very similar to what the late Jiddu Krishnamurti said for decades, speaking of attention, questioning and inquiring, speaking and seeing, dependency, freedom, and unconditioned love. How do you see him and how close do you feel to Kirshnamurti?

TONI. My husband and I went several times to Ojai, California, to listen to K, and we have also heard him speak in Switzerland, and once in England. We never personally met him. It was only after coming in touch with K's work that veils started dropping from my eyes and things became clear. The questioning intensified about what I was doing at a Zen Buddhist center giving talks, holding meetings, participating in ceremonies and rituals, and later being in charge within this formidable setting. The whole question of authority and influencing people burst open and it was no longer a matter of choice that I left the whole tradition. I just had to do it.

You are asking how close I feel to Krishnamurti. When two human beings, you and I, see the same thing directly, wholly, this instant, then there is no longer any question of "closeness." There is no "you" and no "me," no separation of any kind. Something entirely new is functioning freely, and it does not belong to anyone. It is not dependent upon anyone. Is that clear?

JACEK. Yes.

TONI. Was there any other part to this question?

JACEK. How do you see him?

TONI. How do I see him?

I said that it was only after coming in touch with K's work that it became clear what needs to be done. Krishnamurti never ever put his person into the foreground. "The speaker is not important" was his constant admonition. What is important is to see clearly for oneself the truth or falsehood of what is being said. There has never been the shadow of a demand for discipleship or worship. He referred to all of that as "nonsense" and said that it was an abomination to him. Is that enough?

JACEK. Yes, thank you very much.

I have heard one Zen Buddhist monk say that "Krishnamurti was a very slippery fellow" since he did not propose any formal meditative practice. You do offer it at your center. There are seven-day retreats held in silence, consisting of periods of sitting and walking and a period of manual work. You give talks and also interviews called meetings for people who want them. Sitting is optional, but from what I have noticed people rarely skip rounds of sitting. The atmosphere of the sitting room, as you call it, is that of vibrant awareness and purity, in spite of the lack of an altar. The presence of beautiful green plants standing in pots in the center of the room and in one of its corners gives a definite aura of a meditation hall. The etiquette is minimal—no bows, no kyosaku, no chanting, almost no instruments, just a bell signaling the end of a sitting or walking period. During walking you can hold your hands any way you wish, even loose at your sides or in your pockets, yet people move with attentive care and a certain form seems to be arising. When I described it to George Bowman, he commented: "No matter what she calls it, if there is sitting, walking, talks are given, and interviews are held, it is still Zen training." What would you say to that?

TONI. To a casual passerby, some of the forms you are describing might match very closely a textbook definition of a Zen retreat. However, we are constantly reexamining these forms and they do change. We are specifically looking at them from this point of view: Do they provide something conducive to a smoothly functioning, quiet retreat, or have they been retained because of unquestioned assumption or habit?

We state in our information sheet that people may use the schedule in any way they wish as long as they do their daily work assignment and maintain silence. Incidentally, in spite of what you observed at that particular retreat, there are many times during the day when only very few people are present in the sitting room. Also, people can sit on any kind of chair, and they do.

But let me also ask again: Why does one have to compare and pin a label on something that is going on? We do it all the time. But does anything really become any clearer by being named and compared with something else? The important thing is to be directly aware of what is happening in the mind as it is happening—to be aware of comparison, for instance, and to observe its immediate effects. At the instant of comparison, where is the awareness? Hasn't it been replaced by a narrow memory channel that now connects with all kinds of ideas, feelings and emotions?

If someone says, "Toni is still doing Zen training,"—what is that person really trying to convey? Why is he saying it? I can speculate about it, but I would have to talk with him directly to find out.

Whether Krishnamurti proposes any form of meditation or not does not matter to me at all. Again—does one really comprehend what Krishnamurti is saying, or does one project ideas and images onto him for lack of any genuine understanding?

JACEK. I would like to ask you a question concerning sitting itself. I remember Genpo Sensei saying recently during a sesshin in Maine that there are two kinds of sitting—exclusive and inclusive. Exclusive is based on will and striving, with enlightenment as a goal in the future, sacrificing the present moment. It is the practice of concentrating on one point and shunning the senses and the world. There may be an inquiry in it (koan) or not (mantra or visualization). This may lead to a *kensho* experience, but the nature of the human mind is such that it closes up and you start all over again, and this process is repeated ad infinitum. The inclusive practice, on the other hand, is sitting effortlessly, embracing the present moment, looking into whatever arises at the moment, not having any aims and no image of future enlightenment. It is "just sitting," *shikantaza,* as the Japanese call it, with no object and no inquiry. Now you seem to propose the inclusive "just sitting" way, without violent inquiry such as *mu? mu?* or *who? who?* but still with some inquiry, or intimate asking, or wondering, like What is it? or What's it all about? Would you agree?

TONI. I really don't propose anything. When people come for

a silent retreat, we question immediately what is going on in the mind. Why did one come to this retreat? What does one want? It is easy to say: "Don't have any goals, just sit quietly, embracing the present moment without thoughts of enlightenment." But is this what is actually happening? One has to look!

The moment one sits still and attends for brief instants at a time, doesn't the thought of wanting something, and of getting something, arise? It happens. We have been conditioned that way from earliest childhood on and have seen it in others ever since we can remember. "Do something. Be somebody. Get someplace." Or, "Be quiet. Stop fiddling. Don't do this. Don't think. Don't want this or that. Just be in the moment."

Can there be awareness of this running stream of thoughts, commands, reactions, desires, goals, without judgment, without reacting for or against? As long as I am wrapped up in what I want or should not want, wanting itself does not come into awareness. The wanting is just running its habitual course. What *is* wanting? Can we see?

Do you see the difference between wanting something, and the actual process of wanting as it manifests throughout the mind and body? I always come back to the question: Is one wondering how the mind actually functions from moment to moment, and if so, can one begin to attend quietly, in all simplicity?

Does this clarify your question?

JACEK. Partly, because I would like you to specify what kind of inquiry you advocate since you advocate questioning and inquiring.

TONI. I am not *advocating* any kind of questioning or inquiring, but I am inquiring. You, or anyone else, can participate in this—it is open to anyone.

JACEK. How should one carry on the questioning?

TONI. Can there be awareness this instant that the brain is asking for a *how*—a method to latch on to? Do you see that? Can there be simple, quiet observation, silent listening to what is actually happening this instant?

Listen! There is breathing, isn't there? Let's just listen quietly for a moment. Inhalations and exhalations don't need to be counted, they don't need to be called "inhalation and exhalation," they don't need to be concentrated on. Breathing doesn't need to be known in any way. Just simple listening. Not saying to oneself, "I am breathing," or "I am aware of my breath," or "I know what it is," but listening wordlessly, inwardly, without knowing.

Is this separate from the sound of birds? A car? An airplane? The moment we "know" the sound, the instant the brain reacts with naming, with liking and disliking, there is separation—many separate sounds, and *me* separate from what I hear. Can you see this?

Listen again—just openness without knowing.

JACEK. Yes, this is clear—the observing, unknowing mind. But the question is, what kind of questioning may take place?

TONI. I don't know what kind of questioning it is. It is just questioning, wondering, inquiring, listening openly. No prescribed method! The moment you find a technique, you become attached to it and there is no longer any open listening. The mind clings to methods because it finds safety in them. Real questioning has no methods, no knowing—just wondering freely, vulnerably, what it is that is actually happening inside and out. Not the word, not the idea of it, not the reaction to it, but the simple fact.

Anxiety arises . . . will one immediately react by "knowing" it from previous times and bracing against it? "Oh, not that again— I hate it—it's going to get worse, how can I get rid of it?" and so forth. Simply meeting it as for the first time, attending quietly, feeling it, letting it move on its own, revealing itself for what it is without any interference by the brain.

JACEK. Your last booklet bears the title *Seeing Without Knowing*. A certain Zen master frequently uses the phrases "don't know mind," and "clear seeing," but he insists that clear seeing cannot be attained without koan practice. Now you say that all systems condition the mind. You work with people allowing them to bring their everyday problems and to work on them—the koans of their own lives—and you work by looking at that together, but don't you feel that a certain Springwater Center jargon or conditioning can emerge in this process?

TONI. Of course it can. It does! As to the statement that only through koan study can there be clear seeing—how does anybody know? Why does one make such a claim? On what basis?

If one is trained in koan practice one will advocate this method, and if one has had a different training one advocates that. We propagate what we think we know. It is safe. But truth cannot be known. It is as simple as that. Insight, truth, clarity, enlightenment—whatever word you may give to what is unnameable—is not the effect of any cause. It has no method, no training. It has nothing to do with the conditioned, trained mind. So why condition people's minds by saying: "Do this practice in order to attain enlightenment?" We all want clarity and safety and wonderful experiences because we feel so utterly empty, insecure, and afraid. As long as we are afraid and wanting, we are totally vulnerable to ever-new programs and exploitation.

JACEK. Yes. It seemed funny to me that this Zen master came to his enlightenment (he writes about it in a book) by chanting a *dharani,* but it seems that for him the most valuable tool finally is one that works for most people, and in his opinion it is koan training.

TONI. What is a koan—what does it mean to work on a koan? If a koan is just a single word like *mu,* working on it means voicing it (audibly or inaudibly) on the exhalation, trying to get totally absorbed in it to the exclusion of everything else, even to the point of self-forgetfulness, using it to shut out distracting or disturbing movements of the mind—straining hard not to let go of it day or night. Working in this way, the mind is clearly not in a state of open, choiceless attention.

Other koans are statements, descriptions or dialogues that are incomprehensible and perplexing to our conditioned, fragmented way of thinking. The thinking mind cannot gain insight into them. Many koans are the very expression of a mind in which the deceptions of self-centered thinking are clearly revealed and dispelled. The beauty of a koan is the beauty of mind without the limitation of self. Thinking about it cannot touch it. So the question is: Can a koan be seen and understood directly, without any sense of duality, division? In this way it reveals its meaning.

Our way of living, since time immemorial, has been a series of contradictory, perplexing, incomprehensible events created by the fragmented, self-enclosed, conditioned mind. Except for brief moments of pleasure and joy, we have existed in conflict, strife, violence, and unspeakable sorrow, at the same time yearning for peace, harmony, and happiness for ourselves. We have not clearly understood the root cause of this dilemma. What is it? Can it be resolved? Does this question concern us profoundly? If it does, will there be the energy to find out? Can one begin to watch how one actually thinks, speaks, reacts, emotes, and interrelates in actuality and in fantasy?

When the mind is in an acute state of questioning, not knowing—what difference does it make whether it is a koan that is questioned or this very instant of reality? What matters immensely is seeing, not any object of seeing.

What I have observed with koan work in myself and others is that it hooks so deeply into our already conditioned programs. One uses the koan as means to an end. It can also be used to have something to do while sitting—something to occupy the mind rather than face present difficulties. A Zen teacher once said to me: "If people didn't have subsequent koans to work on after passing their first one, they would leave the center." What is this mind, what is this instant when there is nothing to do, nothing to look forward to, nothing to hold on to?

While working on koans, does one seriously and continuously look at the feelings of accomplishment and pride that may be generated by passing a koan? Is one aware of this? Koan work has a built-in system of rewards. It ties in with our age-old feelings of success and failure. Does one continue to depend on the teacher who passes or rejects? Is one in awe of the teacher and senior students who have already passed all these koans?

Does one see the emerging feelings of elitism? Of having something others don't have, or not having what others do? Is there ambition and competitiveness among koan students—comparisons about who passed which and how many koans? These comparisons take place among students and teachers alike. It happens when we get involved in any system. Can one become aware of this in all simplicity and humility and be done with it? If not, self-centeredness, strife, violence, and sorrow will persist, no matter how many koans are seen through.

So—whether the work is a koan or any other problem—is the mind clearly aware of these traps?

JACEK. Do you believe that our personal problems can carry us beyond our personal ego to that point of silence and emptiness to which koans are supposed to lead us?

TONI. Our personal problem *is* our personal ego and it leads us around in circles. Emptiness and silence aren't a place to be reached by methods. Nothing can lead to it. Quiet and empty states of mind can be induced through different practices, but we are not talking about induced quietness and emptiness.

Something entirely new comes into being when the brain, together with the rest of the organism, isn't mechanically engaged in wanting, striving, comparing, fearing, suppressing, attaining, advocating, defending, following, believing, and so forth. It is not a question of getting rid of these movements, but seeing without a shadow of deception what is actually happening inside and out.

Can the vast, running-river mind slow down, come to a halt? Not practicing to halt it, but *seeing what is there* and ceasing to be swept up in it? If we human beings do not understand ourselves freely, profoundly, from moment to moment, there cannot be any intelligent, loving, and compassionate relationship among us. Division and sorrow will persist. Is this clear?

JACEK. Yes. Thank you. Now the next question. Some people in the Zen orthodoxy may label you as a spiritually confused, disoriented, ungrateful, arrogant heretic stealing the tools of their trade and trying to outdo even the most radically iconoclastic worthies of the past. They may claim that you propose the lowest form of Zen—not aiming at self-realization. What would you say to all this?

TONI. I don't know what to say. What people label me and say about me is their own business. We love to talk about other people, put them down or elevate them. Why? Can we watch, as we gossip, praise, or criticize, what it is in us that craves to do this, why it feels so satisfying and exciting, feeling superior while putting down somebody else? What good is it? I am not trying to evade your question—so if you want to bring up some of these things again I'll respond to them.

JACEK. Yes. People put you down saying that this kind of practice does not aim at self-realization.

TONI. What do people mean by "self-realization"? A powerful experience that will settle our daily problems? Awakening to a state of nirvana, bliss, ecstasy? Is that what people believe it to be? I am asked about this all the time. We all have read so many accounts of enlightenment experiences and one wants that same experience for oneself. One will give anything for it, practice any method, follow any teacher.

What is self-realization if not the immediate, moment-to-moment insight into the processes of the human mind? Can fear and wanting be instantly seen and directly understood—not just the present feeling of it, but seeing the root cause and the inevitable consequences that follow? Not thinking or speculating about it, but a penetrating awareness that dispels what is seen? This seeing, this undivided openness, has nothing to do with any experience. There is no experiencer in it—no realizer, no recipient of anything. It is something entirely new and unknowable.

JACEK. Wouldn't you say that what you are doing is "natural meditation"? I can't find a better word now for meditation . . . a natural process through which you want to get rid of all the embellishments and all the techniques and all the traditional forms, allowing simply the natural process of becoming aware to happen?

TONI. Yes. But are you still trying to represent to yourself conceptually what it is that Toni is doing . . . is that what's going on? You have to look whether this is so.

JACEK. I am doing it for the sake of this interview.

TONI. Is it just for the sake of the interview? Be sure you don't answer too quickly, but see whether there isn't tremendous security when we label something, when we know something, when we feel we have established some kind of order. But it's only the order of words!

Your question was, Are you doing "natural meditation"? I don't know what you mean by "natural." I don't know whether we can be natural. What *is* it? This word has become rather abused these days, hasn't it?

What is it that impedes the flow of living lovingly, intelligently, compassionately? Is one interested? Will one watch and find out?

JACEK. Recently you have decided to drop even the word *Zen* from the name of your center and to use simply the name Springwater Center. Do you feel that by doing this you are severing your last connection to your former teacher and the Zen patriarchs?

TONI. The ties to tradition and teachers were severed long ago. The reason that the word *Zen* was dropped was that even though we were using it in, let's say, a "generic" way, it remained a "brand name." In many people's minds Zen is firmly associated with its specific tradition, with Buddhism, with Japanese cultural patterns, or just something "oriental." There is either attachment to the name and what it stands for, or people do not even want to come to this place because of their negative associations with Zen. Incidentally, even though we have registered our name just as Springwater Center, we are adding "for meditative inquiry and retreats" wherever needed. Springwater is the place, geographically, where the center is located. With this beautiful word we don't have to look for any other.

JACEK. Toni, I may be a nasty, aggressive interviewer, but I am really curious. Do you think that you will continue reading from Huang-po, who seems to be your favorite of all Zen masters, in your new phase?

TONI. I don't know what I'll do in talks. In the past, on the last day of retreat, I have read from Huang-po. The last few retreats I didn't do it. I cannot anticipate what will happen in the future.

JACEK. I would like to come back to the koan question. You say that all koan systems condition the mind. You work with people allowing them to bring their everyday problems, the koans of their everyday life, and you look at that together. But don't you feel that a certain Springwater jargon or conditioning may emerge in this process?

TONI. It does. When there is no immediate attention, the mind moves automatically in conditioned tracks. And it is subject to new conditioning. That is so.

Are we just *talking* about seeing, or are we actually *living* with attention and loving care? If this is a vital question then there is the energy to look and listen and discover for oneself.

JACEK. In recent years, several women teachers have radically transformed the male-dominated, authoritarian teaching style within the Buddhist traditions. You have left it altogether. This seems to coincide with the emergence of the repressed feminine side in the minds of the American people. Do you share Soen Sa Nim's belief that in the near future the Western societies will be ruled and dominated by women [*both laugh*] . . . the spiritual teachings included?

TONI. I have opinions, but I don't like to engage in opinions here—I think it's beside the point. I am not predicting what the future will bring. Unless there is a profound change in us right now, the future will be very much like what is going on today and has been going on in the past. Who dominates whom alternates, but can one discern in oneself the tremendous drive to dominate or to be dominated? Whether we be male or female, can we ask the same question: Where do our actions and reactions come from?

Are we living up to culturally conditioned images of "male" and "female," "masculine" and "feminine"? Are we trying to replace old images with new ones? Do we speak and act out of anger and resentment, reacting to being oppressed by others, or to having oppressed others?

Can action spring out of no images at all—just the fullness of being that includes both the masculine and the feminine? All past revolutions have perpetuated the general patterns of power, dominance, and submission in one form or another, haven't they? So, in trying to do something entirely new, are we just reacting to old patterns, which will assure their continuation in a new form, or does action come out of the clarity of no attachment to any pattern, just seeing clearly what needs to be done?

JACEK. Not reacting . . .

TONI. Not reacting! When there is inattention, we automatically react out of the limited concerns of our own fragmented point of view.

JACEK. Now this whole issue leads naturally to the next question. Not only women have challenged the excessively "macho" style of Zen training, the style in which, as George Bowman says, "you grit the teeth and harden the heart." There are several male Zen teachers who teach in a gentle way, truly caring about their students. I am thinking here of various other teachers I've come in contact with. I also don't want to speculate about the future too much, but it seems that this is the next phase after the first, which frequently was so triumphantly self-righteous and authoritarian.

TONI. Authoritarianism and self-righteousness emerge and reemerge whenever there is inattention. When there is inattention, ego functions automatically, self-centeredly—that can be observed. Love and care are not tied to gender. Love and care are not the property of the female or the male—they are not part of the conditioned personality. If it is a learned behavior pattern, it is not love. Any *conditioned* care and gentleness can change into violence and hatred when circumstances change. What was once "love" has now turned into hatred and resentment. I think we can all observe this within ourselves and in each other. Unconditioned love and caring depend on no condition or training, not on whether one is man or woman. They flourish in the absence of self.

JACEK. So you would not agree with C. G. Jung, who used to say that compassion has its roots in the feminine? He pointed out that in most traditions the cult of the female goddess or bodhisattva was necessary to complement the cult of the masculine side. Many people say nowadays that the repressed feminine energy is coming to the fore because we are living in an unbalanced, overrationalized, dictatorial and violently repressive age where compassion and love are absolutely necessary in our relationships if we are to survive on this planet. Of course compassion has no gender, of course those were men who created many of those cults of the feminine, fearing the overmasculinization of their religion, but it still seems true that this gentle, feeling, compassionate side is feminine in character although it acts both in men and women.

TONI. What do you mean by saying that it is "feminine in character"?

JACEK. It is attributed.

TONI. Why does one say that gentleness and compassion are feminine in character? Is one explaining one concept with the aid of another? What is femininity? What is compassion?

Some of the most beautiful sculptures of the Buddhist and Hindu traditions cannot be labeled male or female. They express something beyond stereotyped images. And yet a statue is an image. What is compassion beyond all images?

JACEK. A different question. Do you think that it is possible to transcend a given tradition and yet act from within it? Isn't that what Bankei or Sri Ramana Maharshi did? Some of the early itinerant Chinese Zen masters seem to have had a similar approach. Do you feel that your way of leaving the tradition is the only way?

TONI. I don't really know what Bankei, Ramana Maharshi or the itinerant Chinese monks did. I can read their words, but whether or not they left the tradition is not my problem. It is often pointed out to me that if truly great teachers did not leave their tradition, what arrogance and ingratitude it shows in me to have left it. Of what use are comparisons? Don't they instantly lead away from the work at hand?

If one really needs to find out the cause of human division, violence, and sorrow, doesn't one have to work empty-handed, free from the accumulation of any kind of knowledge? Tradition is accumulated knowledge. A seeing mind does not know—it understands the limitation of all knowledge.

You ask whether I feel that my way of leaving the tradition is the only way. What do you mean by "way"? It is not a way from "here" to "there." I did not leave tradition as a matter of protest or principle, but because any kind of authority, any kind of following, any adherence to what is known, remembered, and cherished does not reveal truth. There is no way to it. Therefore there is also no "only way." Truth is not found by striving for attainment of a goal in the future, but it has to do with questioning, wondering, and seeing *what is* this instant. And . . .

JACEK. And where it leads us we don't know.

TONI. We don't. We don't. The moment we become preoccupied with where it leads us . . .

JACEK. It's a fictitious answer. . . .

TONI. Yes, and there is no awareness of what is going on right now.

JACEK. There is no readiness to let go.

TONI. There is escape into fantasy about the future. So I am not engaged in comparing what we are doing here with what other people are doing. If other people wish to compare, that's up to them, but can one detect comparison in the mind and see the effects of comparison in our daily life, in our relationships? As long as I compare myself with you, with an *image* I have of you, how can I be in direct touch with you?

JACEK. Thank you.

Jacek later wrote:

Since the interview several questions have come up. Would you be so kind as to answer them in a letter form?

I can easily understand that the authoritarian ways of imparting teachings in most religious traditions condition the mind, preventing it from questioning and freeing itself from the weight of the past, visions of the future, and self-importance gained in the process. But many valuable things are passed over from one generation to another, for example the way we sit in meditation. The discovery of adequate sitting postures took humankind thousands of years. Some anthropologists claim that people must have started discovering meditation during the upper Paleolithic period. On steatite seals found in the ruin of Mohenjo-Daro dating from the times of the Harappa civilization (in India, third millennium B.C.) we see human figures sitting in lotus postures with straight backs, and the accompanying symbols point to some deep meditative experiences.

Recently two fine Native American Indian teachers taught a three-day workshop here. I must say that I was deeply moved by their clarity, intelligence, and warmheartedness. The Senecas call meditation "entering into silence." Incidentally, your Springwater Center is located on the former grounds of the Seneca tribe. Is the "seeing without knowing" practiced at Springwater directed solely at experiencing the freedom of non-ego and living in harmony with human beings, or may it also help to see the ways of nature, the energies of the stars, the earth, the plants, the animals, and the spirits, and living in harmony with the whole universe as the Senecas tried to do?

Now, if the members of the Springwater Center start seeing the wondrous powers of nature's energies and begin conversing with plants, animals, and the spirits of the ancient Seneca shamans, will you discard it as obstacles to clear seeing, or will you see it as helpful to living and dying on this planet?

Maybe my question is premature and impossible to answer now. So, if we are moving into the unknown, let's move into the unknown and be with it!

Dear Jacek,

When a human being is sitting quietly, motionlessly, listening out of the depth of silence, does it make any difference what posture is taken, who taught him or her how to sit, what tradition the teacher calls his or her own, how ancient it may be?

I think this does not matter at all. What matters profoundly is that a human being discover directly, clearly, the enormous depth and weight of psychological conditioning that shapes and controls every move of the mind and body, keeping it divided and in conflict with itself, with other people, and with the natural environment. Not just to discover this conditioning, to become aware of it from moment to moment—as it functions automatically, habitually, mechanically—but to wonder whether it can slow down and come to a stop in silent understanding.

Such questioning and quiet attending is not directed toward the attainment of *any* experience—be it a blissful meditative state, the experience of silence, freedom, harmony, power, or seeing "the ways of nature, the energies of the stars, the earth, plants, the animals, and the spirits."

It has nothing to do with seeking experiences, but with directly discovering and unveiling the seeker, the meditator, the wanter, the doer, the experiencer, the keeper, the transmitter—having profound insight into the infinite disguises of the idea and sense of a separate self.

The emergence and blossoming of understanding, love, and intelligence has nothing to do with posture or tradition, no matter how ancient or impressive—it has nothing to do with time. It happens on its own when a human being questions, wonders, inquires, listens, and looks silently without getting stuck in fear, pleasure, and pain.

When self-concern is quiet, in abeyance, heaven and earth are open. The mystery, the essence of all life, is not separate from the silent openness of simple listening.

Awareness Free of Context

*Awareness cannot be taught, and when it is present
it has no context. All contexts are created by thought
and are therefore corruptible by thought. Awareness
simply throws light on what is, without any
separation whatsoever.*

Dear Toni,

Even though I am very drawn to you personally, I have decided
not to continue working with you. I want to work with people
within a Buddhist framework.

I realize that you indicated during last year's retreat that you
were not a Buddhist and that your organization might drop the
word *Zen* from its name. I told myself that this didn't matter
because you seemed to teach true Buddhism.

During the retreat this year, and despite the hospitality of people
in Springwater, I felt disturbed by something I could not identify.
In part I think it was the double message I experienced. For
example, Springwater denies any affiliation with Buddhism and
yet most of the forms used at the retreat come directly from the
Zen tradition.

I began to realize, particularly after the retreat, that I do not
know what your fundamental assumptions, experiences, and goals
are. What is the context within which you teach awareness work?
For example, I would really like to know whether you experience
these things to be true: the Four Noble Truths, the Eightfold Path,
the precepts, the nature of form and emptiness as expressed in the
Heart Sutra.

Part of the change in my relationship with you certainly comes
from my acceptance of the fact that you do not wish to be identified
with Buddhism or any other tradition. Last year I projected my

---

This chapter contains a letter to Toni from March 1987 and her response.

desire for a Buddhist teacher onto you and tried to make my projection fit. Curiously enough, other people who listened to your tapes experienced the same confusion as I. People assumed you were a Buddhist despite your denial of this.

I don't think that all of this comes from "distorted internal images," though some of it has. I also sense some change in you and in your teaching since last summer and in comparison with tapes from earlier years.

All of this is to say that even though I will not continue my membership at Springwater, I value my relationship with you and would like to stay in contact.

Thank you for the work we have done together.

Dear ____,

In your letter you talk about being disturbed by something of a "double message" at Springwater: on the one hand the denial of any affiliation with Buddhism, and then on the other hand there are cushions, a wooden block to signal time,* and a schedule that includes meetings and a talk, all part of the external form of a traditional Zen sesshin.

I'm not sure that you want an explanation from me, and yet you are raising the question. So let me state that I left a traditional Zen center because it was impossible to question within that context the totality of our conditioning, including the traditional forms and beliefs themselves. We do question the forms we use in retreats at Springwater and drop or change what has been found unnecessary or in need of change.

You ask: "What is the context within which you teach awareness work?" Awareness cannot be taught, and when it is present it has no context. All contexts are created by thought and are therefore corruptible by thought. Awareness simply throws light on what is, without any separation whatsoever.

You want to know whether I experience the Four Noble Truths, the Eightfold Path, the precepts, the nature of form and emptiness as expressed in the *Heart Sutra,* as true. No formulations, no matter

---

*The *han,* or wooden block, is no longer used at Springwater Center.

how clear or noble, are the Truth. Truth is inexpressible in symbols. The question is: Can a human being see directly, understand immediately (which means without any mediation) the origin of sorrow in herself or himself? Can one see and understand directly and immediately what perpetuates conflict and division in oneself and others? Can one see and understand directly, without mediation of any kind, the ending of suffering in oneself?

Isn't the first step on the Eightfold Path right insight, which is free from the sense of a separate self, a separate experiencer or thinker? Without right insight, how can there be any right speech, action, meditation, and so on? As long as the sense of self divides us, the following of a path or precepts perpetuates that very self.

Why did the Buddha say in parting, "Be a lamp unto yourself—take only the Truth for your refuge"? Why do we seek refuge in things created by thought and memory?

I may be wrong, but human beings communicate, commune with each other freely and lovingly only when the mind is not anchored in any system whatsoever—when there is a coming together empty-handedly.

All the best to you.

Attachments to Groups

In facing our own deep-seated need for security and belonging, can we see the immense attachment and dependency on groups and organizations? Can we see the need to feel that our *organization,* our *religion is superior to all others?*

Someone asked in a meeting: "Why do you knock Buddhism? You seem to imply that Buddhism is just like any other religion, which clearly it is not. Take, for instance, the present situation in Iran—the terrorism, violence, and brutality emanating from that Muslim country. If it was a Buddhist country, things surely wouldn't be like that."

First of all, there is nothing to "knock" about the sayings of Buddha. His teaching was to understand oneself profoundly, clearly, wholly—to see the truth about "self," its inevitable sorrow, and go beyond. Buddha admonished his listeners not to accept the spoken word, nor tradition, nor what is written in a scripture, nor another's seeming ability, nor the consideration, "this person is our teacher." "Be a lamp unto yourself," were the Buddha's parting words, "betake yourselves to no external refuge. Hold fast to the Truth. Look not for refuge to anyone besides yourselves."

How can that be knocked?

The vital question remains: are we actually *living* that way?

When this center was started, the question was whether profound insight and understanding could take place without a traditional religious context of any kind. Could one drop all traditional rituals, ceremonies, dogmas, symbols, hierarchical structure, lines of transmission, teacher homage, and veneration, and just carry on with fundamental questioning and awareness?

Our deeply rooted sense of "self," of "me," inevitably breeds feelings of insufficiency, anxiety, loneliness, and insecurity. Con-

---

This chapter was adapted from a talk delivered in July 1985.

sciously or unconsciously we sense the danger of our separation and isolation and therefore cling to something that appears greater and more stable than ourselves. Attachment to something greater provides a delusive feeling of security and protection. Further, it results in a pleasant feeling of self-importance and pride.

With this ever-recurring process in individual human beings, the separation of humanity continues—separation into exclusive entities like tribes, nations, religions, spiritual and political movements, and so on. All this brings about internal and external division, conflict, rivalry, violence, war, and endless sorrow. It has gone on like this throughout human history and is still happening this very day. Look at the bloody confrontations in Ireland—not by members of two basically different religions, but by mutually exclusive adherents of the Christian faith. Look at the Middle East, where followers of three major religious traditions are cruelly at war, and these groups have splintered into even smaller factions that are at each other's throats. There is religious warfare going on amongst the formerly "nonviolent" Hindus, the Muslims, and the Sikhs. There is violent persecution of the Hindu population by the Buddhist population in Sri Lanka. It is happening throughout the world because we human beings divide ourselves into national, ideological, economic, racial, and religious fragments.

With any division into groups there inevitably arises the feeling: "The group is *me*." The validity of the feeling is rarely questioned (as the validity of the "self" is rarely questioned). It feels so real and serves so well to delude oneself into a temporary sense of permanence, security, and importance. The self is made more substantial through the group. If "my" group is attacked, I feel personally attacked. I feel impelled to defend the group and retaliate against the offender. One will even give one's life for the identity bestowed by one's group, worldly or spiritual. The brain seems programmed that way.

What is our response to this? Do we accept it and go along with it? Or do we see the urgent need to question national, ideological, and religious divisions of any kind?

Is the particularly intense violence that flares up in one country due just to that country's specific religious tradition? Or is it a simple fact that human beings the world over are violent? The Christian institution of Inquisition, with its greed for property and power and its brutal incarcerations and tortures, lasted several centuries throughout Christian Europe. The torture and murder of millions of human beings of different races, religions, nationalities, and political convictions in concentration camps and prisons the world over has not come to an end. Fighting and hurting each other for the sake of idea and identity, as well as power and supremacy, is an indiscriminate human disease that keeps flaring up in all parts of the globe—yesterday in one place, today in another, and tomorrow elsewhere. It will continue as long as we human beings remain fragmented entities attached to self-image and group identity, which cut up the whole of humankind. It will continue as long as we live in ignorance of what we actually are thinking and doing to ourselves and to others from moment to moment. It will continue as long as we remain unaware of the fact that we *are* the "others." The mind that is Muslim, Buddhist, Hindu, Sikh, Christian, or Jewish is the same divided human mind.

So what are we to do?

What are our usual responses? Can we watch these carefully? Are they an escape from the fact?

When we label some people as "Muslim terrorists," what does that do to us? In our own daily relationships, do fear, anger, violence, and the desire for revenge arise constantly? If we become aware of this, do we immediately look for excuses and escapes, or is there a free facing of the fact?

In facing our own deep-seated need for security and belonging, can we see the immense attachment and dependency on groups and organizations? Can we see the need to feel that *our* organization, *our* religion is superior to all others? And can we see what that does to us?

The question always comes up: What about *this* organization? Doesn't it, too, generate feelings of belonging, attachment, dependency, and division?

Yes, it may. Nothing and no one is exempt from the danger of creating attachment and dependency.

No one can drop fear, attachment, and dependency for another. It has to happen within oneself. It is for each one of us to discover the power and incredible danger of attachment. This does not mean forcing oneself into not being attached, but to *see* attachment,

and its causes and consequences, clearly in oneself. Can it drop
effortlessly?

The idea of cutting loose brings up anxiety and fear and a
strong urge to justify the attachment. Group support and religious
sanctioning of the attachment provide the security we are looking
for.

Is it possible not to follow such escapes?

Can we go to the root source of fear and anxiety, not seeking
security, not knowing how it will all end?

Can one allow total insight into this whole process to give birth
to a new way of being? A way that is not fragmented?

When this center was founded, we wondered if we could work
without creating a new organization. It seemed that the best way
to avoid the entrapments of organizations was not to have one in
the first place. As it turned out, incorporating and naming the new
center was a legal necessity. For a while we wondered if we could
avoid creating a "membership." We finally agreed that because of
the need for financial support for a place to sit, meet, and hold
retreats, and for a staff to keep it functioning, the term "member"
would simply refer to someone who is interested in the work and
who contributes to its costs on a regular basis. It was also agreed
that people who did not provide regular financial support would
not be excluded from the activities of the center. That's all.

It is for each individual to observe with utmost care what
actually happens within oneself the moment one calls oneself a
"member" of an organization. The question is brought up time
and time again.

Is membership connected with a new image, a new identity that
distinguishes itself from "others"—from "nonmembers"?

Does membership imply feelings of ownership? And of follow-
ership? Is one using membership or participation in the group to
satisfy personal motives and ambitions? Has one become attached
to the place, the people, the teacher, to the extent that any
disturbance of what one has become used to constitutes a threat to
one's feelings of security?

Can all this be seriously questioned without starting from any
conclusion or prejudice?

Only when there is no division, no sense of self, can love and
compassion come into being.

Tradition and Separateness

What am I, what are you, what is every one of us anywhere on this globe when all images, identities, and traditions are put aside?

Dear Toni,

I enjoy chanting, be it in Japanese, Korean, Tibetan, or English, just as I enjoy singing or dancing. I like the smell of incense just as the smell of the forest, and I am moved at the sight of beautiful Buddha or Bodhisattva figures in museums, just as by religious art of other traditions, or fine human faces reflecting a noble and intelligent mind. So I feel comfortable within the Buddhist tradition when experienced in a humane, warm way with no authority trip and no unnecessary intellectualizations, and I also enjoy your questioning, "formless" teaching, just as Krishnamurti's.

Dear _____,

I am interested in your statement about feeling comfortable within the Buddhist tradition, and the reasons you give for it. I can well understand your appreciation and enjoyment of chanting, dancing, of Buddhist and other art forms, of the sight of a beautiful, intelligent face, and the smell of the forest. As for incense—isn't its wafting, smoky fragrance linked in the human consciousness with the idea of sacredness—memories of thousands of years of burnt offerings? What remains when associations in the brain are clearly seen and disconnected?

There is a difference between affirming one's personal (or collective) enjoyments and comforts, and seeing directly the havoc that divisions have created on this otherwise so beautiful earth.

This chapter contains excerpts from a letter to Toni in July 1986 and her response.

These divisions are manifold—we are born into a family, a clan, a nation, a race, a linguistic heritage, a religious belief, and so on and on. Being aware of what is going on in every part of this world in the name of ideological identity—whether national or racial or religious or any other—can we continue to participate?

It's not a question of renouncing chanting, incense, or figures, nor continuing with them because they are precious, enjoyable, and comforting. The real concern is whether it is possible to see what we human beings are doing—the total picture—even if it threatens our personal inclinations and attachments.

I may feel sincerely that I am not causing harm to anyone, even that I am helping others with my private and collective activities and identities. But what is the root of the interminable strife and suffering of human beings, be it in the Beiruts, the Northern Irelands, the Sri Lankas, the South Africas, or our very own backyard?

It may not bother me to see someone salute his flag as I salute mine—but can I begin to question every instant of human conditioning? I may be convinced that the symbols and rituals of my choice do not hurt anybody, but do I see the worldwide, millennia-old mutual destruction engulfing human beings in unspeakable hatred and sorrow? Not just explain it, but discover the root source of it in myself?

People have said to me: "Buddhism is not the problem. *Attachment* is." But would there be any "isms" at all if there was no need for attachment?

How can we even begin to glimpse our deeply anchored attachments as long as we cherish and defend all that we ourselves have created to satisfy our longings and allay our fears?

What am I, what are you, what is every one of us anywhere on this globe when all images, identities, and traditions are put aside?

One may have glimpses into the unfathomable wholeness of all life, but so quickly this becomes interpreted and propagated in terms of the particular tradition one is identified with. That is the separation! Do you see that? What am I, what is everything, when tradition ceases to be the source of energy and security?

Are these purely theoretical considerations, or can one allow such questions to operate deeply, gently, freely—shedding light on our day-to-day, moment-to-moment living?

Seeds of Division

*Can we question why we need to be something—
Buddhist, Christian, Muslim, Jew? What is that
something? Is it a thought, an image, a concept
about oneself? Having a concept about oneself is a
divisive thing, isn't it?*

TONI. A peace fellowship—but why "Buddhist"? Why can't
we come together as human beings? Why do we have to come
together as Tibetan Buddhists, Theravadins, Vipassana practition-
ers, or Zen Buddhists? This is still reaching out from within our
small boundary lines.

LENORE. I understand what you're saying, and ideally, ultimately . . .

TONI. But I don't say, "ultimately."

LENORE. You say now!

TONI. Do it now.

LENORE. What would you do now?

TONI. Drop it!

LENORE. How do you do it?

TONI. I can only do it myself. Not for someone else. Maybe in
talking with people who want to find out about themselves, who
are already deeply troubled by division, this dropping of separate
identities takes place. Then we don't need to reach hands across
walls because there *is* no wall.

LENORE. Part of what has been so important to those of us
who have been working this way is things we've learned from the
Buddhist tradition that help us *not* perceive boundaries, *not* perceive barriers.

This dialogue took place during an interview by Lenore Friedman with
Toni Packer in November 1983. The discussion was about Lenore's work
with the Buddhist Peace Fellowship.

TONI. Can you give an example? What can you learn from a tradition—you don't mean intellectual learning, do you?

LENORE. I guess I mean . . .

TONI. Is it ideational?

LENORE. Certainly not *only* ideational. But there is ideational support of, for example, nonduality.

TONI. Have you learned that?

LENORE. I hope so. Well, I'm *learning* it.

TONI. Is it here? Is it so *now?*

LENORE. It infused a lot of the work we did—or at least that was what we were working for: to at every moment see when duality arose, and let it go.

TONI. But do you see that duality arises with your calling yourself a Buddhist?

LENORE. Does it have to?

TONI. How can you avoid it? There are also Catholics, Protestants, Muslims, Jews, Hindus, Sikhs, and the fighting is going on right now, all over the world. How do you look at these confrontations that happen everywhere, the killing in the name of "my" religion and "your" religion?

LENORE. They seem a total violation of what religion is all about.

TONI. And yet it's going on. It has gone on ever since there have been such divisions.

LENORE. Do you see *danger* in what we're doing?

TONI. Yes, to the extent that this reinforces, supports, or in any way maintains my identity of being "this" in distinction to "that." All such self-images separate and divide.

What I want to find out is: *What is peace?* Is there really such a state as peace? True peace. Harmony. Wholeness.

When that is there you don't need to join a movement trying to bring factions to peace. Factions cannot be peaceful. When you're apart, there cannot be wholeness.

Can we question why we need to be something—Buddhist, Christian, Muslim, Jew? What is that something?

Is it a thought, an image, a concept about oneself? Having a concept about oneself is a divisive thing, isn't it? It fragments the mind.

LENORE. What form could we conceive of that would *not* fragment or divide?

TONI. Why do you have to conceive of *any* form?

LENORE. Well, because I'd still like to work with these people! We're working well together in a way that would be consonant with the kind of things you're saying. But we don't have to call ourselves . . .

TONI. We *don't*. I want to be very sure from moment to moment, observing carefully, honestly, what by-products identification of any kind yields me psychologically. Because it does yield something; watch it for yourself.

If you realize profoundly that you are all humankind, then whoever you are working with, you're working with all humankind! We all have this same mind—the mind of ideals, of hope and fears, of striving and ambition, of goals and frustration, of anger and kindness—the whole stream of self. Can one—one human being—really see this clearly, instantly? This seeing, this insight, is without duality, without division. No division in one human being—what happens when this one comes in touch with others?

But as long as I come to you as a Buddhist and you're a Catholic, there's already division. Oh, we may stretch hands across the border and call each other sisters and brothers and yet we both hang on to our identity because we can't let go of it. These divisions are the things that are blowing us up. The nuclear bomb is only a by-product of that.

LENORE. I know you're saying that applies to what I'm doing—with the Buddhist Peace Fellowship—that the same principle applies.

TONI. Yes. At least I would question, "Am I contributing to this stream of division and separation?" You can only take responsibility for peaceful action in yourself—and that takes a tremendous amount of honest inward looking. People have done vigils facing the United Nations building. Why do you have to sit in that particular direction? If you're not sitting in *all* directions, which means *no* direction, it's a fragmented approach to a fragmented problem.

LENORE. Do you really think they felt they were sitting in one direction?

TONI. Well, physically they were. What was going on in each individual I don't know. In reports I've read there seemed to be quite a bit of self-consciousness about sitting there on the pavement with all the people passing by, being aware of one's erect posture and how this might impress passersby, maybe hoping it would have an effect. This is all dualism, a reinforcement of self-centered thinking. The mind is so deceptive! We put ourselves into a new posture and position and the little monkey mind continues its old work.

LENORE. It isn't perfect, but . . .

TONI. Coming back to what you're trying to do—and you're trying to work not just superficially but profoundly . . . Let me ask: This work you're doing together—this work for peace—does it really impel a human being to question deeply what is peace and what is war within oneself? And the connection between oneself and "the world"?

LENORE. I hope so.

TONI. But is this the *overriding concern?* Because this is where war originates—within oneself. It's not just a mass phenomenon "out there"—*we* do it! We're the cause of it. If this isn't clearly understood in oneself, how can it be settled on a global level? It is within oneself that the work has to take place, primarily.

LENORE. Is it the only place?

TONI. This question comes up frequently—do I have to be perfect before I can work with other people?—and of course this is absurd. One works, whether one goes to a peace fellowship meeting, stays with the children, or carries out a job. And as one works or rests, is there clear awareness of how one thinks, feels, clings, identifies, prejudges and stereotypes people, and so on?

LENORE. And what if we had those questions going, all of the time?

TONI. Are you asking: "Then does it matter whether we sit in a circle or in front of the UN?" I'm asking: "Are we, while sitting, also planting seeds of division by identifying with a group?"

LENORE. I don't know the answer to that. I'd like to keep that as a question.

TONI. Yes. This is the way. If we answer it, then we don't keep it as a question.

Hurt and Defense

When there is hurt, can energy gather in undivided awareness—very, very still, open, undefended, vulnerable? When that awareness has a chance to operate freely, it's an incredible discovery. It is not necessary to defend! What is hurt and defended is memory!

One of the haunting problems of every human being is hurt: getting hurt, having gotten hurt before, the dread of getting hurt again, and all the defensive measures that the brain and the organism take to protect themselves from past, present, and future hurts.

No retreat goes by without our questioning with all the passion and intensity that's there: What is it that gets hurt when we get hurt?

Can we look at the whole process of getting hurt with a great sense of urgency right as it happens, questioning what is going on, being with it, allowing it to unravel and reveal itself completely? The moment we get hurt, can there be instant looking and listening?

But getting hurt continues mostly *un*questioned, and with it arises the automatic defensiveness and protection against the hurt. Is there fear of facing all of it directly at the very moment? Or, at times, is there a glimmer of awareness of what is happening? There may be, but is it immediately followed by thinking and feeling, "I don't want to be in touch with all this painful stuff?" The dread of facing hurt, of living with hurt, of going through it, and the fear of hurting someone else while caught in one's own hurt keep the body-mind locked in pain and numbness, in conflict, and in an incessant search for escapes. So, right now, can we devote as much time and energy as it takes to look at hurt?

This chapter was adapted from a talk delivered in April 1989.

The brain may say, "I don't feel hurt right now, so how can I look at it?" But hurt is usually not very far below the surface. Memory can evoke it quite easily.

Investigating it, one's first impulse usually is to find an explanation for why we got hurt and what caused it. The brain is always searching for explanations of what happened and why it happened. Since that seems to be its favorite way of investigating, can one let it go ahead, yet give close attention to what is happening in a broader, more encompassing way?

The brain not only hungers for explanations, for finding causes, but also for protecting and defending the image it has built up of "me." It protects and defends the "me" by finding fault elsewhere. Can one see this as it is taking place? Looking for a "cause" of the hurt, finding one in the recent or distant past and then explaining, justifying, defending, blaming, lashing out, or withdrawing into a self-protective shell—all of this takes place in thought, in fantasy.

The brain can continue for hours, days, or years going over internal videotapes and sound tracks, playing back what happened, why it happened, and what could have happened or should have happened instead. This way it remains entangled in a loop of fantasy with its pain, emotion, conflict, and withdrawal. It's all part of the hurt. Are we together on this? Can one look carefully at all of this, not just read over it quickly?

Does awareness of the whole process cut through the entanglement?

Let's start out freshly. Someone criticizes me harshly and it immediately hurts. Why?

Being criticized brings up all kinds of thoughts and feelings about myself in the presence of the other—feeling embarrassed, humiliated, rejected, guilty, worthless, or whatever. One may instantly feel threatened, endangered, condemned, and cut off from safety, approval, and love. (There are lots of other feelings like anger and vengefulness, but let us keep it as simple as possible.) The thoughts and feelings that come up may vary from one person to another, from one case to another, but they are *there,* affecting one's total state of being.

Now, is it possible to go deeper?

Is one in touch with present as well as past hurts that are instantly triggered by memory, not only mental, but also physical, organismic memory? Present feelings of hurt automatically plug into painful memories that have been stored in the brain and throughout the organism since earliest infancy. The human brain and body accumulate and store those memories indefinitely, mostly unconsciously. In activating old memories, the body feels just as pained, afraid, and angry *now* as when those incidents happened years ago. Memory evokes all that—one can experience it directly for oneself.

All of us, without exception, were hurt as little children many times over, and memory-traces of these hurts and their accompanying circumstances and reactions are stored throughout the whole organism. At one time or another a loving mother or father was not there when needed. At one time or another we were misunderstood, scolded angrily, admonished with threats, punished, embarrassed, ridiculed, or humiliated. Not all of this may have happened to us directly; the imprint may have come by feeling the violence done to other members of the family or community.

We adults usually aren't aware of what we are doing when we are angry, exasperated, or exhausted. We all have had violent reactions programmed into us since time immemorial. We automatically perpetuate what we have learned to imitate and store in memory since earliest times: the tone and quality of the voice, the bodily gestures, the look in the eyes, the furrowing of the brows and other facial expressions. All of that has been conditioned—learned through imitation from many sources long ago when we were children ourselves. One can observe older children scolding younger children in exactly the same fashion that they have been scolded.

So having been hurt by a loud, angry voice (which is a trauma to the infant organism), having been put down harshly, forced to do something in a painful, humiliating way, not just by parents but by other powerful persons, all of that hurt is deposited in physical memory. It is not merely deposited, it is the operating force.

Hurts are also recorded as unfinished business that is constantly nagging to come up again. The reaction, "An eye for an eye, a tooth for a tooth," is a deep-seated program in our repertoire of automatic responses. So, getting hurt and paying back the hurt are the most intimate of twins. They go together. But the important thing is not just to understand this intellectually—to get the idea of it and explain it to someone else—*but to observe it directly as it operates in oneself.* If that doesn't take place, nothing changes fundamentally. Hurting and getting hurt continue.

We are examining hurt and realize that there has been hurt since the earliest days of our lives. We may not consciously remember the specific incidents, but it is a fact that the intensity of the present hurt reverberates with the recordings of past hurts. Can that come into awareness?

One may have been astonished on some occasion that one got terribly hurt over a trifling incident, but the entire past history of hurts reverberates in this present hurt. It is manifesting *right now* in all the feelings, thoughts, emotions, fears, pains, and tensions. Can one see all of that immediately as it is happening? Can one see the chaotic impact that a trifling incident is having right now? Someone criticizes me harshly, and I feel as though doom is closing in. To the helpless child, contact with a violent, punitive person spelled some kind of doom, and all the reactions of panic and defense that came up were instantly recorded in brain cells and body tissues. An incident happening now that is reminiscent of a past one instantly mobilizes all those connections.

Can there be awareness of this total process as one is on the receiving end? Not escaping from hurt, thinking *about* it, withdrawing from fear and pain, but allowing the situation with all its physical symptoms, feelings, tensions, and pressures to reveal itself for what it is? Not running away from it but pausing instantly to feel, look, and listen?

That's only possible when there is no escape into the intricate defense system that has grown over the years to protect oneself, or rather to protect the *idea* of oneself. The organism itself isn't threatened, is it, when we are criticized harshly? So what is threatened? Can that be questioned instantly? Where is the danger? What are we protecting? Is self-protection the problem? Can the energy of awareness break down the walls of defense?

Have we come to the core of what gets hurt when we get hurt?

Defense means isolation, the absence of relationship. One cannot be well defended and at the same time be sensitive, be in intimate, vulnerable touch with everything. That's very clear, isn't it? It holds true for one single human being as well as for a whole nation.

We don't know from our whole past experience that it is all right and survivable to be undefended. We don't know that. Everything we have ever done, heard, observed, and learned from experience is to defend ourselves, not only physically, but psychologically as well. (We're not questioning the need for intelligent protection of the physical organism. We're questioning the need for psychological defense.) We don't know that we can exist without this defense. As helpless infants and children we got hurt psychologically, and defenses started building up automatically. Now we are living that recording like a tape running continuously—endlessly hurting or else growing numb to avoid the pain. Apparently the brain cannot or does not differentiate between intelligent protection of the organism and protection of the accumulated memories of oneself. It mobilizes to protect memories just as it does to protect the body from physcial harm.

So, what is undefendedness?

When there is hurt, can energy gather in undivided awareness—very, very still, open, undefended, vulnerable? When that awareness has a chance to operate freely, it's an incredible discovery. It is not necessary to defend! What is hurt and defended is memory! It is possible to hear the harsh criticism with complete attention, see and feel what is getting hurt or about to get hurt, and *not* defend.

Is it possible to get to this point beyond all explanation and intellectual understanding? It is *actually* being without any defense. It is dying to the deeply ingrained urge to save the "me," leaving aside, without any effort or purpose, the defense that presses to come up from sheer habit. Defensiveness doesn't have to go on—that's the miracle!

It may feel like being out on a limb. It has never happened before because defense is so habitual, so trusted, yet so isolating and painful in its consequences. But nothing new can happen while being entangled in defense and protection.

So, looking at it, wondering about it—can there be at the moment of hurt the spark of attention that disconnects and holds in abeyance our automatic past? Taking the risk of not knowing how this will come out, but not defending. Not developing a new technique—we're not talking about a technique. Technique is defense. Rather, it is just being vulnerable without knowing the outcome.

There is nothing to defend. When this is as clear as a cloudless sky, life is without the hardness and friction of shells. We're warm, soft, live beings capable of listening to each other freely and touching each other deeply. Being in complete touch with each other means the absence of all division between "me" and "you." It is the absence of hurt and defense. It is freedom.

Freedom from Images

It is a simple fact that this work can only start with oneself. When images dominate the mind, motivating our actions and creating goals of what we want to be or become, confusion reigns. How can we resolve confusion in the world if we are confused ourselves?

It is a fact that one is a woman or a man. Also that one has an image of oneself as a "woman" or a "man." Not just one image, but a whole host of images. That one is a "Buddhist" is an image. That one is an "American" is an image, apart from the fact that one carries some papers when one goes abroad. If one looks carefully, to think of oneself as an American, a Buddhist, and a woman is to be tied up with images, emotions, and feelings of separateness.

Before I left to come to the conference, I was asked a question by a woman who was working in the Springwater Center kitchen. She had dropped in a short while before, and has been active in the women's movement. She asked me, "What are you going to say to these people when you go? Are you just going to talk about this or that, or are you going to be concerned with women—how they have been downtrodden in spiritual traditions and placed at the bottom of the hierarchical structure, how men have considered that women are incapable of enlightenment, which holds for different Buddhist traditions? There are women who are waiting to hear about this. Are you going to address yourself to this? What are you going to do about it?"

The work of questioning deeply into the human mind is more than concern for specific issues, or specific problems. The whole

In September 1984, Toni was invited to the Providence Zen Center Conference on Women in American Buddhism. This chapter has been adapted from an article in the February 1985 issue of *Primary Point,* a quarterly journal of the Kwan Um Zen School.

human condition is embraced. This work is not doing what we normally do and have been doing for hundreds of years: rushing to solve problems in a more or less violent way. This work is to *understand* a problem, not just superficially, or even deeply, but totally. It is to understand so completely that the problem may be resolved through this understanding and not through any "solution" at all.

Before continuing, let me say something about listening— because we are from many different backgrounds, places, countries, traditions, or "no tradition." How does one listen to a talk like this? Can you listen carefully as though it was just a conversation between you and me? How are you listening? Do you have an image of Toni?

To my surprise, a number of people here have said, "I know about you. I've heard about you." So do you have an image? Knowing about Toni, having an idea about her, maybe you've read a little booklet, heard stories, and now you have an idea of what she is or propagates. And does one have an image of oneself, of the group or tradition one belongs to? Is there the ever-readiness of the mind to compare what is being said to what one already knows? Then one is not listening. One is comparing, and what is actually said flows by unheard.

So, at least for the short duration of this talk, is it possible to suspend what one knows, to suspend comparison? Can one just be open, completely open, not knowing how one will react, just receiving? If one has an image of oneself or of this person who is sitting here, pure listening is impeded or distorted. One reads into it or subtracts from it, or one will not want to listen to some things at all. It may be too painful or too threatening.

Do you see that you do have an image of yourself as being somebody or many "bodies": a Buddhist, a woman, an American? When the Olympic games are shown on television, for example, there may be a strong appeal to the "American" image. Does one simply watch the screen or also watch what goes on in oneself? When an American stands on the top step to receive the gold medal, with the national anthem being played and the Stars and Stripes raised, does one's patriotic heart feel a boost? A boost to what? A boost to an image! And perhaps if one's country has won lots of medals, one doesn't mind seeing others win one too every once in a while, because one is also identified with the image of "brotherhood." As far as one's religious affiliation is concerned, is one identified with it, attached to it, so that one's self-image is invested in the religion, the religious tradition or the center that one belongs to? This can easily be tested. When someone criticizes one's religion, does one feel defensive immediately, personally attacked and hurt? Or if someone praises one's group or center, is one's vanity flattered? One's personal vanity, one's identity—"this is *me*."

And as a woman, what kind of images does one nurture, maybe quite unawares? Many people say to me that women have such a negative image of themselves, that one has to work on this bad image, improve it, empower it, which means substituting a good image for a bad image. But why does one need *any* image? Can we see the difficulties, the impediments, the separation that all images create within ourselves and between each other?

One may well have witnessed the battle of inner images: One wants to be a good mother, but one also wants to go to retreats. There are guilt feelings about one's duty as a mother, and guilt feelings about neglecting one's spiritual side. Furthermore, one wants to be respected as a woman pursuing an independent career, doing something more than just mothering or housekeeping. So there is a battle of images within that may express itself in general frustration, in overworking, or in resentment. In interpersonal relationships too there is strain; two people living together, having images about themselves and about each other, inevitably create conflict. One may see oneself as the victim of domination when one wants to dominate oneself. So who dominates whom? One feels manipulated and has a need to manipulate others because one has been manipulated oneself.

Watch it for yourself. You will discover amazing things that go on in this mind and therefore throughout this body. Anything that goes on in this mind, a single thought, is totally connected with the whole organism—electrically, neurochemically. One pleasurable thought gives a gush of good feeling. Then one wants to keep that feeling, which is another thought: "How can I keep that?" And when it stops: "What have I done to lose it? How can I get it back?"

The poor body has to respond to all of this: It is not even done with the pleasure and already there is pain. It takes the physical organism a while to get back into balance. I don't know whether our bodies even know what balance is anymore. There's so much old residue held within the body, within the brain.

We do all this mental bookkeeping, we remember what someone did to us this morning, yesterday, a year ago, sometimes ten or fifteen years ago. "I'm not going to forget that," we say, which means no fresh and open relationship with the person is possible. The person is branded, marked. We see him or her and there is the image of what he or she did. Our response is dictated by the image, dominated by it. When there is an insight into this whole process, the seeing is already the interruption of it. Nonetheless, image-making may immediately continue because it's very pleasurable to us. We live in and for our images, even if they're painful, because we think we have to live for something.

Can one question all this? I don't call this work "Zen" anymore, because the word is extra, unnecessary to the inquiry. This fundamental inquiry into the human mind and body (not *my* mind and body personally, but the human mind) doesn't need any descriptive label. To the extent that this mind, as it functions in images, blockages, contradiction, and conflict, is clearly understood, the whole human mind is understood, because it does not differ fundamentally from one person to another. On the surface we're all different, but fundamentally each of us has an image of being a self, of being someone.

To see that this is an idea, a thought creation, seems inordinately difficult. The self-image feels so solid and real, that one takes the self for a fact. One confuses it with this body and the ongoing processes of thought, sensations, and emotion. But there is no owner of all this.

To say "this is me" and have an image—"I'm good at this, I'm poor at that"—is a mental construction, thoughts and ideas just like all the others that make up the stream of thinking. Yet "this is me" is the root of all our individual, interpersonal, and international problems.

Most people are very concerned with the state of the world, the terrorism, the fighting that goes on in the Middle East and elsewhere. I once heard a famous news commentator report about a new violent incident in Jerusalem where Christians, Muslims, and Jews are at bloody loggerheads with each other. He said, "How is it possible, in the place where three of the greatest religions were born, all of them preaching peace, that people kill each other? It's unfathomable." But if one thoroughly understands identification, investment, image, defensiveness, and aggressiveness by seeing them directly in oneself as they happen, then it is not unfathomable that members of different groups fight each other and even kill each other.

So what is one going to do about all this? Here again is the question asked of me by the woman in the kitchen: "What are you going to do about it?"

It is a simple fact that this work can only start with oneself. When images dominate the mind, motivating our actions and creating goals of what we want to be or become, confusion reigns. How can we resolve confusion in the world if we are confused ourselves? We just carry our confusion with us in whatever we do. Will we start to look, to question everything, and leave no stone unturned, which may shake up our whole foundation?

We may anxiously or defiantly keep our images and feel, "I can't do without them, I'm attached to them. It's human nature." But can we be clear about what we are doing? Can we see that our foundations are made up of separation and isolation, because they are divided from the foundations of other human beings? We're all defending our own foundations, believing in them, taking refuge in them, and at times reaching as if over the foundation walls to shake hands with others, who in turn reach over their walls to shake hands, all of us assuring each other verbally of our mutual understanding. But the walls remain intact and division continues.

Can these walls break down completely, so that nothing separates us from one another? It is a tremendous challenge. You may feel I am exaggerating, that this is just my opinion. I'm not trying to give opinions. Can we look seriously into ourselves, and see the dangerous consequences of identifying with something or somebody, the danger of being "somebody"?

It's only when one really works on oneself, probing deeply and stopping nowhere, that one gets in touch with this fundamental anxiety of being nobody. And usually there's an immediate withdrawal from that anxiety. The human mind wants something to which it can cling. But will one not escape this time? Will you face the anxiety—just raw anxiety? Not stopping the questioning, but simply feeling, listening—quietly, with no goal in mind. Just being with what is there or isn't there, in utter silence.

Maybe there is a flash of insight into the fact that we are nobody, nothing. With this comes a joy that cannot possibly be put into words. It has nothing to do with words. It is no image, no thought.

Then in the next moment do we try to hold on to it, and make it again into an image? "I am somebody who has seen. I'm somebody who knows." Do we congratulate ourselves? Who is congratulating whom? Do we try to recall and relive the experience? Images come so quickly, like mushrooms springing out of the ground on a warm moist day. There they are—new images. Can they be seen immediately and dropped instantly?

Or does one just carry on in thought: "I've done this thing. I've broken through. This is it. I'm no one!" What does it mean— "I'm no one"? It's already become a concept, a memory.

So, is it possible to see and be free of images from moment to moment, really being no one and therefore completely open and related to everyone and everything, with a lovingness that cannot be produced through any kind of practice? Love is not practiceable. It's either there or it isn't, and it is *not* there when the "me" is there who wants to bring it about, who tries to grab it and hold on to it.

One may deceive oneself about being a loving kind of person, being very compassionate. Is it just an image? Does one see when it comes up? Can it be dropped instantly so one really does not know what one is? Just letting action flow out of this not-knowing, just being in touch with what is there—listening, seeing, responding openly?

It's up to each one of us. No one can do it for us.

Listen!

Form and Absence of Form

Maybe one will sit forever and never come upon the truth! Is truth dependent upon sitting? Upon correct posture? Upon anything? It is dependent on nothing. That's the beauty of it—it depends on nothing. It has no cause, no method, no attainment, no preservation. What is it?

We usually think that we are dealing with personal problems peculiar to ourselves. But this is an illusion. If one scratches beneath the surface coating of personality, all people have very similar fundamental problems: problems of fear, of desire, of anger, of time, of wanting, of attachment—all problems of the "me," the self.

Questions often come up about the "form" or absence of "form and discipline" in which we work and move during our retreats. These questions have been put to me off and on ever since I left a Buddhist Zen center and we established a new center. "Why don't all people here hold their hands during sitting and walking in the traditional Zen way, which surely has very good reasons like keeping the energies flowing evenly, uniting the opposites, bringing about a uniformity of movement in the hall, lowering the mast of ego," and so on?

In asking such a question, is one free to examine where it comes from? Does it arise out of dependency on a system and the defense of this system? Or has one actually tested out the truth of all these claims that are being made? Can one actually know the truth of it, or is one just repeating what one has been told again and again?

It is the very identification with a system—as comes up with the word *Zen*—that brings about separation, conflict, and violence among human beings. The shared feeling of having something

This chapter has been adapted from a talk delivered at Roseburg, Germany, in December 1985.

better, something superior to others, is common to religious and secular organizations. A Zen teacher once said to me: "If you didn't have the deep conviction that *your* religious tradition was the best of all, you wouldn't belong to it. Why not be proud of it?" Out of this pride of specialness arises the division into "mine" and "yours," "better" and "inferior." Also, frustration and anger arise when others in the fold do not do exactly as I am doing. "They are indulging their ego while I am controlling it. If I have to do it, why don't they?" and so on. With conformity comes the violence of comparison, enforcement, suppression, and punishment of deviants. Do you see that? Do you see the danger?

But back to the hands. Maybe you have never tried out whether one position of the hands is better than another—maybe you don't want to bother with that, nobody says you have to. But one thing is clear: When there is a freely flowing energy that has nothing to do with "me," my desires, my fears, my failures, and accomplishments—this energy is not tied to any posture of the hands, feet, or back. It is tied to nothing—it is simply there in abundance, in the snow and ice, the sound of the wind in the trees, in the stillness and movement of all life.

On the bare branches of trees there are little buds, tightly wrapped for the winter. On a warm spring day the covers suddenly burst and there are tiny new leaves, ever so delicate and vulnerable and yet so resilient. This is the energy of life, of which we are an integral part when we are not thinking that we are apart.

Discipline is something that human beings have practiced since time immemorial—the discipline of obeying, conforming, imitating, subjugating oneself, and marching in equal step. Why do we do this? It is practiced in monasteries and in military systems the world over. As I was growing up in Germany, in 1933, everyone had to start walking in equal step. The images of this uniformity—the uniforms, the enthusiasm, fanaticism, compulsion, and violence of people conforming—made a profound impression. Tremendous feelings of comfort and safety are provided by a system in which one does everything one is told. One does not have to think for oneself, one need not question and find out for oneself. It is so much easier to follow. Does one see the danger?

Somebody said in a meeting: "I see people putting their hands in their pockets during walking, or just letting them dangle loosely at their sides. Do they do this out of rebellion against the old traditional forms—just to prove how free they are?"

Each one has to question and look for oneself. Is there reaction, rebellion in what one is doing? One cannot assume that one is *not* rebelling, that one is free from old systems and new systems. Can one simply see what is there?

Is it possible to keep the hands in any particular way and not have an image or idea about oneself? "I'm a seasoned Zen person." "I am free from this Zen stuff." "I do zazen in the proper traditional way and they don't." Images and ideas about oneself and about others *do* come up all the time, don't they? One can see it clearly when there is close attention. Can one see it happening and cease being influenced? Can one sit, stand, or walk without becoming somebody by assuming a posture?

This question cannot be answered by thinking about it. Opinions are worthless. One has to watch very carefully what goes on in the mind as the body assumes conditioned or rebellious postures. If one has any opinion, one cannot watch freely. Opinions distort perception.

Can we become aware of our insatiable urge to speculate about why other people do what they are doing? Why are we so concerned about what *the others* are doing? Is this concern preventing us from realizing what we ourselves are doing this moment?

Somebody asked: "Why are you still sitting?"

Whom is one asking? Who knows? I cannot speak for anybody else. One has to pose these questions to oneself. Not answer them on the spot out of one's cherished opinions, but observe intimately, from moment to moment. Why is one sitting? Does sitting itself help to question, look, listen, and clarify?

In traditional Zen centers that work with sitting and posture methods, it is often said: "Just sit long enough, and eventually, maybe after many lifetimes, you will come upon the truth." It is also said: "Sitting in the correct posture itself is enlightenment." Is one attached to these ideas?

Maybe one will sit forever and never come upon the truth! Is truth dependent upon sitting? Upon correct posture? Upon anything?

It is dependent on nothing. That's the beauty of it—it depends on nothing. It has no cause, no method, no attainment, no preservation. What is it?

Sitting and sitting postures do not liberate—the brain and body can become just as conditioned and programmed by this activity as by any other. Seeing the truth liberates—not any practice or method. Can one see the truth of what actually is taking place this instant, inside and out?

Can one look at conformity and see what it does in oneself and in relationship with others? Can one observe how one is attached to something, how one yearns to belong, how willingly one obeys what is demanded, how one believes what is preached, how one imitates what is going on in the community one calls one's own? How one goes along, becomes identified, begins to protect, cherish, and defend it, as well as to attack the deviants?

Is it humanly possible to walk alone, without any accompaniment? Not isolating oneself from human beings—I don't mean that. What I mean is without the accompaniment of the constant soliloquies, the running commentaries, the comforting ideas, the hopes, the attachment through thoughts and ideas to people, beliefs, and ideals, the future plans and past experiences?

Can one hear this vast running river as *just that*?

There is an old Chinese dialogue that may deepen this questioning, maybe even shed light. One person asked of another:

"Who is it that walks alone, without any companion?"

"I will tell you after you have swallowed up all the waters of this vast river in one gulp."

"I have already done that."

"Then I have already told you."

Sitting Quietly, Doing Nothing

Awareness, insight, enlightenment, wholeness—
whatever words one may pick to label what cannot
be taught in words—is not the effect of a cause.
Activity does not destroy it and sitting does not
create it.

Recently, during a private conversation someone asked me: "Why is it that you never talk about sitting outside of retreats?" If I understood correctly, the person felt that if Toni, in talks, encouraged sitting, people would sit more, benefiting themselves and the community at large. Further, not publicly mentioning the value of regular sitting may tacitly encourage people not to sit much, so that they miss the precious opportunity to be freely in touch with themselves and their fellow human beings.

I have thought a lot about this. We do talk about sitting and meditation in private meetings and at workshops, but can any broad recommendations ever be made?

Over the past twelve years I have worked individually with many people who are, or have been, involved in Zen practice. It has been illuminating to discover different motives for sitting.

One may take up sitting because one feels some deep dissatisfaction with one's life. One has read or heard that sitting (meditation) can help one feel more energetic, healthy, creative, compassionate, and capable of resolving daily problems. Most of us who start Zen practice have read books containing enlightenment stories old and new, and we have listened to teachers speak about enlightenment, realization, or liberation in workshops, seminars, and talks. One may have a close friend who is a member of a Zen center and has highly recommended sitting practice. To some degree or another one has become convinced that sitting is one of the surest ways and

---

This chapter was adapted from a talk delivered in October 1984.

means to become a better person, maybe even an enlightened one, whatever one may imagine that to be.

Most Zen centers and communities offer group sittings on a regular basis. Very often in such a community it is very important (or even required) to be in the meditation hall at certain set hours. If one attends sittings conscientiously, one may be regarded as a serious and promising student by the teacher and senior disciples. So, in addition to the longed-for goal of betterment or enlightenment, there is the immediate reward of being considered a "good boy" or "good girl."

Participating in sittings, conforming to what fellow members are doing, bestows the comforting sense of belonging and the exhilaration of shared energy. We do like to feel safe and good, and we will make great efforts to attain this feeling of security and righteousness. Conversely, not sitting arouses guilt feelings about not doing what one expects of oneself and what those in authority expect of one. In either case, old habits continue to be reinforced and to dominate one's life, without light being shed on them.

Since there are always newcomers to a Zen community, comparisons arise between "beginners" and "advanced" or "developed" members. Wanting to become like an admired "developed" person, or wanting to join that inner circle, may arouse the energy to strive toward that goal.

Is this any different from what we have done all our lives— imitating and competing with one another in order to advance or become like someone else? Spiritual training can hook right into this preexisting compulsive pattern. Being praised, or praising oneself for making progress, gives satisfaction and the impetus for further striving. Perhaps one becomes oneself an "example" for a beginner. This can enhance one's self-image, flatter one's vanity, lend zest to one's life.

Energies aroused by comparison, competition, and striving direct attention away from what is actually taking place this very instant, and toward the desired goal or reward. This is preoccupation with thought and image—not a free inquiry into the very nature and root source of thought and image.

For some people, comparison with the success of others results in feeling like a failure oneself. If one is ignored, or if one feels frustrated with one's lack of progress, energy may be depleted in discouragement and despair. At this point people frequently abandon sitting altogether.

Most compulsive sitting sooner or later gives way to not sitting at all. It is a common experience. People who depend on outwardly imposed discipline to sit have reported that the incentive to sit disappears when the outer requirements disappear. Also, when no tangible rewards are felt or promised by the teacher for patient sitting, many people lose interest. One may never really have sat with a genuine inner urge to look and to question freely into oneself and to attend carefully and quietly to what is actually going on inside and out. The yearning may have been there at one time or another during one's life, but a compulsive outer and inner structure has not allowed it to operate freely, on its own. If one does start to sit again on one's own initiative, old compulsions and motives may clearly reveal themselves.

It is widely taught and believed that "beginning" students must have outer discipline and structure in order to establish a solid meditation practice. The implication is that at a later time freedom from outer structures and controls will take place by itself. The question is: Does one become inwardly conditioned by outer discipline and structure, continuing to depend on it, finding a safe refuge in it?

It is a fact that as long as one is frightened to stand alone on one's own two feet the compulsive need to follow a system continues. As long as one is afraid of one's inner insufficiency and doesn't face it directly, one remains totally vulnerable to any kind of conditioning influence that offers a semblance of stability and the possibility of being somebody. One keeps clinging to the imposed system, defending it passionately as if one were defending oneself, because one's existence always seems to be at stake. One may vehemently deny being attached to teachers and systems, but one is immediately thrown into a state of anxiety and confusion when both are seriously questioned, or when one happens to find oneself in an environment devoid of the familiar discipline and authority figures. At such a time one may seek and find another compelling teacher and system, or one may actually undertake in all seriousness to delve deeply into this mind with all its hidden fears, demands, and compulsive tendencies.

In almost all young children there is an innate curiosity and joy to examine and investigate everything within reach, and to discover things independently. Even though children need the security of a safe and trusted environment, they also want to be free from outer controls and impositions in their urge to find things out for themselves. Our established ways of bringing up children in the home and schools easily dampen or even destroy children's zest for unfettered exploration and discovery. And yet, if not totally squelched, it can resurface again.

This work of deeply wondering about everything that is going on—wondering who and what one actually is, and whether there may actually be something beyond the endless struggles of daily life—can never be the result of any imposed outward pressure. Pressure only results in more pressure. A free spirit of inquiry isn't the result of anything. It is there, spontaneously, when we are not dominated by systems of inner and outer control. Let me give an example. When one needs to listen to a strange sound, doesn't one naturally stop making noise? One cannot listen carefully as long as one is talking, thinking, or moving about inattentively. The need to listen carefully creates its own stillness. When one actually realizes how inattentive one is and begins to wonder about what is actually going on inside and out, doesn't one *have* to look and listen quietly?

If one needs quiet times for questioning and attending, just as one needs food to eat and air to breathe, no outer discipline is necessary to make one do it. One simply does it. That is the beauty of it.

So, after all that has been said—what is it to sit quietly, motionlessly, together and alone, for long periods or short ones, uninfluenced by what others have done and said, or are saying and doing right now?

Maybe I should stop here and let you answer this question for yourself. Maybe you have already answered it for yourself.

The person who asked me why I do not speak about sitting mentioned that after long periods of sustained sitting day in and day out, something happens within that makes it possible to open up to people and things in a clear and caring way. This person spoke about the sacredness of sitting.

Sitting motionlessly quiet, for minutes or hours, regardless of length of time, is being in touch with the movements of the body-mind, gross and subtle, dull and clear, shallow and deep, without any opposition, resistance, grasping, or escape. It is being in intimate touch with the whole network of thoughts, sensations, feelings, and emotions without judging them good or bad, right or wrong—without wanting anything to continue or stop. It is an inward seeing without knowing, an open sensitivity to what is going on inside and out—flowing without grasping or accumulating. Stillness in the midst of motion and com-motion is free of will, direction, and time. It is a complete letting be of what is from moment to moment.

Sitting quietly, doing nothing, not knowing what is next and not concerned with what was or what may be next, a new mind is operating that is not connected with the conditioned past and yet perceives and understands the whole mechanism of conditioning. It is the unmasking of the self that is nothing but masks—images, memories of past experiences, fears, hopes, and the ceaseless demand to be something or become somebody. This new mind that is no-mind is free of duality—there is no doer in it and nothing to be done.

The moment duality ceases, energy that has been tied up in conflict and division begins to function wholly, intelligently, caringly. The moment self-centeredness takes over the mind, energy is blocked and diverted in fearing and wanting; one is isolated in one's pleasures, pain, and sorrow. The moment this process is completely revealed in the light of impartial awareness, energy gathers and flows freely, undividedly, all-embracingly.

Awareness, insight, enlightenment, wholeness—whatever words one may pick to label what cannot be caught in words—is not the effect of a cause. Activity does not destroy it and sitting does not create it. It isn't a product of anything—no techinque, method, environment, tradition, posture, activity, or nonactivity can create it. It is there, uncreated, freely functioning in wisdom and love, when self-centered conditioning is clearly revealed in all its grossness and subtleness and defused in the light of understanding.

Silence

Can the inner noise be entirely left alone while attending? When the changing states of body-mind are simply left to themselves without any choice or judgment—left unreacted to by a controlling or repressive will—a new quietness emerges by itself.

Our retreats are held in silence so it may be good to say what is meant by silence.

During the seven days of a retreat we do not talk to each other except during meetings that take place about once a day. When there is some kind of emergency in which one urgently needs to say something to someone, people are asked to do so where other people do not need to see or hear it, or they may use paper and pencil to communicate.

You may wonder: "What's wrong with saying a few words here and there, particularly during work periods? It's so much simpler than writing notes, and need not be a distraction if it is done quietly." I am not saying it is *wrong* to talk. We simply agree not to talk during retreats and to see what happens. One may find out that communication is possible without any spoken words—that a much deeper kind of nonverbal communion with the people and all the natural things around us takes place when our habitual verbal expressions and exchanges do not envelop us. Energy gathers naturally when we do not engage in any talking.

Most of our waking hours are spent in talk—so much of it unnecessary and often harmful. While we talk there is rarely any listening space—it is so arduous to talk and listen at the same time. But when the impulse to verbally react and speak out about everything that comes to mind slowly abates, our mental, psychological, and physical reactions come more clearly into awareness.

This chapter was adapted from a talk delivered in January 1984 on the first day of a seven-day retreat.

Outward silence helps reveal the inner noise that goes undetected while we talk and talk.

Can the breathing, the attending, take place in the midst of inner noise? If, at the moment of noticing the constant inner chatter, we immediately think: "I must stop it in order to attain deep silence," these very thoughts are the continuation of the chatter. To say to oneself, "I can do it" or "I can't do it, it's impossible" is more of the same.

Can the inner noise be entirely left alone while attending? When the changing states of body-mind are simply left to themselves without any choice or judgment—left unreacted to by a controlling or repressive will—a new quietness emerges by itself.

I do not mean adopting or imitating some prescribed behavior patterns of the "attentive, alert, quiet, Zen person." Hearing Toni talk about moving and working in silence, one quickly establishes an image about this in the mind and then tries to live up to it. Related ideas about being liked and approved of for this kind of behavior add to its artificiality. This is not attention. It is role-playing, which conditions the body and mind. *Attention* means letting all the noise of one's habitually inattentive, image-ridden ways come into full awareness.

When one is inattentive while opening or closing a door, that is, absorbed in thoughts about being someone special or being some-place else, noise inevitably accompanies the thoughts. Is it possible to be right there with the whole situation, the doorknob in the hand, the feel of it, turning it carefully, not knowing in advance how the whole mechanism really works? This kind of interested attention does not create extra noise. It is not bent upon eliminating sounds. Listening sensitively and caringly to all the sounds we make brings stillness in its wake. One can see this for oneself. The extra noise we just made came out of inattention—having been somewhere else in our thoughts. Choiceless awareness, sensitivity, and stillness go hand in hand—they arise mutually and do not condition the body-mind. Clarity of awareness is freedom from conditioning.

Listening to the sounds issuing from one's footsteps, from sitting down or getting up, putting food on a plate, setting a dish on the table, washing pots, cleaning the sink, or cutting vegetables may reveal how much we actually depend on and enjoy hearing ourselves make noise. Making noise may have the aspect of reassuring us of our continued existence as somebody, often somebody important. Can all of this come into awareness instantly as it happens? What happens when it actually is realized? Does one continue inattentively, blaming oneself for it, feeling guilty, resolving to become more attentive in the future, or does extra noise simply end in clear awareness? It is for each one of us to find this out.

When images about how one should or should not behave, or how things should or should not be, do not captivate and control the mind and movements of the body, there is freedom to attend—freedom to question without knowing. Then the wind in the trees, the sound of rain dropping on the roof, footsteps in the hall, the chirping of birds, the clanking of pots, the barking of dogs, and the passing of a car do not break the silence.

Authority

> *The authority of our past experiences, convictions,*
> *beliefs, insights, and hopes can be just as blinding*
> *and binding this instant as the attachment to the*
> *outside authority of spiritual teachers. Why do we*
> *need to lean on any authority in observing what is*
> *actually happening?*

Dear Toni,

I am more aware of all the judgmental thought processes that go on concerning these spiritual wants of mine. Sometimes I am lost in them, back to comparing old and new, memories of what seemed to be, of a need to repeat something that was titillating. Then there are periods like today when I freely observe what is going on, and the trap is released for a little while. In a dream about a previous spiritual teacher last night I was weeping, wanting. I see that the teacher was, and I guess still is, an attachment that has many facets—a parent of sorts perhaps, but also the kind of authority who spoke in absolutes: "If you do all this, you can get that." It was so very reassuring and continued my dependent need for the very authority that I should have been observing deeply, which I began to do in the last retreat.

Am I willing to accept the great discomfort that comes with being my own authority? And yet every time I look carefully and observe what is going on, I am my own authority. I see, after retreat, that it is not just the watching, without comment, without distraction, the doing of daily things like brushing the teeth or peeling the ripe peach. There is a new dimension here, the watching of all thoughts, the moods, the depression that awakened me this morning, the ennui. Instead of pulling out my former

This chapter contains excerpts from a letter to Toni from October 1985 and her response.

"Zen" dialogue, which goes like this—"This depression is a mind state like clouds in a clear sky, it will pass and leave the clear sky. Patience"—I find myself looking at the depression, seeing perhaps in myself a very deep dependency on teachers and techniques that were to have freed me for all time, seeing that it is all more thought and making a problem out of problem-making.

I think that there is a kind of "training," for lack of a better word, that goes on in these retreats and goes home with one: to continue the observing—replete with fear and dislike.

Part of me wants and needs to get back to retreat in October— part of me wants to move on to another authority altogether. But the latter is too transparent and so now I will simply live along, hoping to be more free than trapped in looking at each emotion and conflict that comes into mind. I will let it just happen without looking for happiness or freedom or safety or serenity or anything at all. This is where it is.

Dear ———,

Not much needs to be added to your observations. Just to be alive and aware, without choice, from moment to moment, without looking for anything.

It is not really a matter of becoming "one's own authority" either. The authority of our past experiences, convictions, beliefs, insights, and hopes can be just as blinding and binding this instant as the attachment to the outside authority of spiritual teachers. Why do we need to lean on any authority in observing what is actually happening?

Isn't it our anxiety, our constant search for escapes, and our deep-seated resistance to facing and questioning every single move-ment of the mind that create this longing for authority? It seems to be so much easier and more soothing to let someone else take care of us—tell us what to do and what not to do, evaluate where we're at, what progress we have made, and what attainments await us in the future. Our unresolved fears and cravings for psycholog-ical and spiritual refuge and security bring all authorities into existence. If human beings face fear and pain directly as they arise, discovering their very root source and dropping all escapes—where then is there need for any authority?

Or, to put it differently: Does direct, undivided attention to what is going on inwardly and outwardly need any authority? Don't all present and past influences have to stop interfering completely in order to attend fully, immediately, and wholly? Only then can there be the stillness of pure observation. We cannot possibly attend freely as long as compelling thoughts and re-membrances about what we ought to do or what we have done in the past clutter the mind.

So, it is ever-tempting to slip into our age-old conditioning, looking for promises and rewards like little children, seeking escapes from fear and pain and dreading punishment for "wrong-doing" (punishment for not obeying spiritual authority and tradi-tion). Can this be seen as a powerful habit of thinking and reacting and then be dropped without getting entangled over and over again?

When fear, wanting, depression, and our habitual escapes are transparently clear as they arise, and the source from which they spring is revealed, then the flow of attention will not be inter-rupted. When attachment to inner and outer authority drops away, attention itself is the source of right action. It is right action.

Can the truth of this be grasped immediately?

Or do we make an *idea* of "no authority," so that the very idea becomes a new authority and we are still in the trap?

Effort

Thinking of a desired goal and straining body and mind to attain it take energy. It happens at the expense of being intimately in touch with what is actually present, right now, without any resistance or struggle to change it.

Dear ———,

You write that the rare times you decide to sit with some discipline and focus you notice a different state of mind and feel somewhat more awake and energetic in your daily life. Then the question comes up whether it is OK to make this effort since the remembered advice is, "Don't make an effort." There is a conflict between what you observe directly—that discipline and focus in sitting lead to some alertness and energy in daily life—and what you remember having been told about making an effort or no effort.

If you see the beauty of living energetically and wakefully and find that some disciplined and focused sitting brings energy and alertness, why are you made unsure by what someone else has said? Why is the mind so eager to follow authority? What is said in talks and meetings is not meant to be advice to be followed. It is direct questioning, observing, and finding out for oneself.

So, if one doesn't take anybody's word for the truth, what can one do to find out for oneself? Can one simply attend carefully, learning from moment to moment what is happening inwardly and outwardly?

I want to see directly, for myself, what goes on throughout this mind and body, and not live under the constant influence of what others tell me is the right or the wrong thing to do. I see clearly that unless there is open awareness this instant, mind and body

---

This chapter contains Toni's response to a letter from April 1988.

function mechanically, habitually, according to ingrained patterns and influences.

I realize that I cannot possibly respond wholly and appropriately to people and ever-changing situations if there is inattention. Without careful attention, ancient or newly formed patterns of behavior react immediately and compulsively, and create conflict.

I see that when there is the urge to find out what is going on this instant—not just thinking or speculating about it, but looking and listening *directly,* quietly—the energy to attend is there. It needs no special effort or preparation to bring it about. Questioning and insight generate energy! Unnecessary habitual baggage drops when it is uncovered and clearly seen. There is real joy in discovery!

It is also noticeable that when I use willpower to stay attentive I somehow lose it. Straining to get something or to preserve something for myself immediately changes the effortless openness of an attentive mind into the entanglement of duality. Self-centered concern and openness of awareness don't go together.

You mention that during a past retreat you hardly remember trying to accomplish anything, and that the retreat was most valuable when you were *not* making an extraordinary effort. You are questioning, however, whether coming to the retreat itself, getting up early in the morning, doing a lot of sitting, and so forth, wasn't a special effort in itself. Are you making a problem out of the concepts *effort* and *no effort*? Would it be less confusing to look at how *energy* is used in our moment-to-moment living?

Obviously everything we do, think, feel, say, resist, or repress uses energy. Conflict uses up energy. Wanting something other than what *is*, without clear awareness of that fact, consumes energy. Thinking of a desired goal and straining body and mind to attain it take energy. It happens at the expense of being intimately in touch with what is actually present, right now, without any resistance or struggle to change it.

Of course it takes energy to come to a retreat, get up early in the morning, forego one's habitual mechanical routines, and sit or walk quietly, giving careful attention to what is going on moment by moment. However, attention without judgment or choice is *energy gathering* without the dissipation of struggle and conflict. It is seeing what *is*, without wanting it to be otherwise. *Wanting* to be aware is not awareness. Can awareness shed light on wanting and its conflicting tensions, without thought immediately trying to do something about it? Energy is released and gathered when conflict is uncovered, seen, and dissolved in choiceless seeing.

The energy of attention is there when the mind pauses to wonder about itself and the whole of life—listening quietly, non-selfcenteredly, without knowing.

Making Resolutions

Making resolutions becomes a comforting
reassurance that we will accomplish in the future
what we are not ready to do right now.
Postponement is the perpetuation of inattention.

When a dish comes tumbling down from a shelf and one sees it happen, the hand immediately stretches out and catches it. Falling, seeing, and catching are one complete action.

If the mind is caught up in dreams, the falling dish may be seen too late or not at all, and before the hand reaches it, it has already crashed to pieces. Saddened and annoyed over the loss and over our own negligence, we may resolve to become more attentive in the future.

We make promises, resolutions, and vows because we have been brought up to believe that this will help somehow. We believe that if we commit ourselves through words, we are more likely to do what we think we ought to do, or become what we want to become in the future.

But is this really so?

In the case of the falling dish, is it saved because we have previously resolved to become attentive? Or does awareness function freely, actively, and intelligently when the mind is unpreoccupied?

In resolving to become more attentive, or to reach a state of complete awareness, an ideal goal is established in the mind. A division in time occurs: One's actual present negligence is separated from the idea of future attentiveness. Thinking of a future goal is an escape from our present discomfort and dis-ease that arise from inattention. We much prefer to think about developing into a better person and following a method to get there than to face the

---

This chapter was originally published in July 1983 in the *Genesee Valley Zen Center Newsletter.*

pain and root cause of our present insufficiency. Making resolutions becomes a comforting reassurance that we will accomplish in the future what we are not ready to do right now. Postponement is the perpetuation of inattention.

Another division occurs between myself as a judge and the action that "I" condemn. "I" condemn "my" negligence as though "I" and the "negligence" were two separate things. Are they really?

Can one carefully examine all this? Not just take someone's word for it nor immediately react against the words. When there is a deep feeling of responsibility for everything we do or don't do from moment to moment, attention and questioning come naturally.

If there is a great urgency to find out something, the energy is there to attend. Faced with a critical emergency, we usually attend and act with our total being. At the instant of immediate danger, past resolutions and future goals are completely irrelevant. There is only the seeing and acting appropriately, without choice.

Why do we go back to sleep once the emergency is over, satisfied with the vow to wake up some time in the future? Why don't we respond immediately to the ever-present danger of inattention? Do we see it?

Once the dish is shattered, can one see the whole situation inside and out as it is, without the excuses, the blame, the regrets, or the resolutions taking over the mind?

And then sweep up the pieces and discard them.

Thinking and Awareness

*Thinking cannot resolve problems. The energy and
clarity of seeing do. Can the pressure to achieve
results come into direct awareness as it arises?
Without immediately wanting to do something
about it? Wanting to have a remedy of any kind is
the separating veil.*

Dear _____,

Let me quote a section from your letter before responding to it.
You say: "The thinking process wedges itself between myself and
reality. It is as though thoughts give rise to a veil that makes clear,
direct seeing impossible. Is it correct that in such situations only
equanimity and patience will help?"

Let us look at it. Thoughts come up. Do they wedge themselves
between an entity ("myself") and something called reality? What
is this entity? What is reality? What is the "veil between"?

Clear seeing reveals one unitary stream of thoughts. "Myself,"
"reality," and "in between" are images, parts of that thought
stream. Clear seeing is completely independent of thinking, but
not necessarily incompatible with it.

So the question is: Do thoughts come out of the clarity of seeing,
or are they produced by ideas and motives? For instance: Has the
desire to attain something produced thoughts? "Attainment" itself
is a thought.

Does one seek security through thinking?

Does one want to get rid of the veil of thoughts in order to
experience clarity?

Can motives, goals, expectations, and judgments come into clear
awareness? At the instant of seeing clearly, the entanglement in
thoughts is revealed and begins to dissipate.

This chapter contains excerpts from a series of letters between Toni and a
correspondent from July 1984.

As to your question, whether equanimity and patience will help when one finds oneself in a fog—equanimity and patience without awareness and insight do very little. Without direct awareness of the processes of the human mind, the unconscious pressure to hurriedly get rid of problems (like the veil) is compulsively at work. The pressure to get rid of problems springs from thoughts and therefore does not dissolve them. Thinking cannot resolve problems. The energy and clarity of seeing do. Can the pressure to achieve results come into direct awareness as it arises? Without immediately wanting to do something about it? Wanting to have a remedy of any kind is the separating veil. Do you see that?

Dear Toni,

After receiving your letter I began to ask myself what attention really is, or rather: "What is going on when I am *not* attentive?"

Until now I had always thought that this matter was very clear. But when I began to look and observe directly what was happening, I found to my surprise that I wasn't clear at all about what attention really is.

Catching myself being inattentive during a sitting, and intensely observing what was going on, I found that inattention is the automatic proliferation of all kinds of mechanical thought and image patterns, like the playing of a phonograph record. In this connection, let me tell you about a recent experience that impressed me very much.

I telephoned my mother and she began to talk about the past, particularly about an incident when I was a baby and she had given me a little whack on the bottom for having spit in her face. She had told me this story many times before, always laughing a lot while relating it. During the telephone conversation she started on it again and I thought: "Well, here it comes again." I leaned back and simply listened to her from a certain distance, as it were. The story and the different laughters seemed to be perfectly known to me. At times I had a sudden, disturbing feeling that there was a phonograph record on the other side—a kind of automaton was repeating something. A strong feeling of estrangement arose within me.

All in all, with these experiences during sitting and in daily life, my understanding of awareness has drastically changed. Until then I obviously had had merely an intellectual conception of what constitutes awareness. Now, with these new insights, it seems above all to be . . . here I hesitate. I think that anything else I could say right now would merely be a play with words.

During a recent sitting I took up a question from your book: "What is complete attention?"

Asking this simple question has helped me and a few others very much. I think I have learned that if one pursues this simple question with intensity, one discovers entirely new dimensions of awareness. Sometimes, if one is really awake and attentive, one experiences the entirety of life, including its trivial details, with a sense of wonder.

Then I have frequently observed in myself something that is difficult to describe: Maybe I could say it is as though out of limitless vastness and freedom—a state in which there is just this sense of wonderment at everything—something is pulling back together, narrowing down. A tightness comes back and one gets stuck everywhere—one is no longer free.

Right this moment I am questioning: Why does this narrowing down keep occurring again and again?

During the past few days I have experienced something like that again. I had been thinking about the consequences of my Zen work in relationship with the patients I work with. Somehow the idea had occurred to me that if I personally continue to develop, there would also develop increasing distance between myself and the patients—I would understand them less and less.

Fortunately, during sitting last night it became clear that this "distance" is also an idea—obviously an idea that results from "I"-centered, egotistical images. It is this "I" that creates the distance in order to feel better, cleverer, more developed, or whatever. Surely the idea of a reward for the long and arduous work of sitting has played a role in this. After all, one wants a reward for this sitting and the reward is that one is happier, better, and more "developed" than the others!

I ask myself: Why does it happen that this "I"-centered thinking and imagemaking always forms anew?

It seems to be like this: If one imagines the process of Zen work to be a development, then on every new step a new "I" crystallizes that has as its content the memory of past experiences. Carrying on with the work of sitting, questioning, and attending dissolves this "I" again.

Peace Fellowship

*In working for peace, if that is what I am doing, do
I understand deeply, inwardly, that peacefulness and
self-centeredness cannot coexist? That when the self
is in operation there can be no inward and outward
harmony?*

Can we ask, what is peace fellowship?

In looking at it, it is clear that there can be peace fellowship—peaceful, harmonious relationship—only if no self-centeredness is separating me from you. When we are free from self-centeredness, there is the immediacy of mutual caring without conflict. Conflict arises as soon as my selfishness collides with your selfishness.

We human beings derive a precarious sense of security and pleasure (as well as pain and sorrow) from the sense of self. This sense of self is not confined to images and feelings about our own individuality, but includes whatever else we may be identified with—persons, groups, titles, possessions, ideas, religious and political beliefs, and so forth. It gives one a feeling of importance and security to be identified with something larger, greater than oneself, and therefore this something assumes great importance. One invests in it, cherishes it, upholds it, defends it, and fights for it—singly and collectively.

Understanding this profoundly, can one convey to people that there is no security in self-centeredness? Can one convey that self-centeredness is at the root of war? That our cherished group identities, in which we seek security, are also the cause of violent confrontation and collision?

Since there are innumerable different individual and group identities, we live in self-created isolation with its division, contradiction, and violence. This is clearly in evidence everywhere. Is

---

This chapter was first published in April 1984 in the *Rochester Buddhist Peace Fellowship Newsletter.*

peaceful fellowship possible as long as the search for security through self-image and identity with something greater divides the mind? When there is no self-image and no identification with anything, what is there to be made secure?

In working for peace, if that is what I am doing, do I understand deeply, inwardly, that peacefulness and self-centeredness cannot coexist? That when the self is in operation there can be no inward and outward harmony?

Are the people with whom I come in touch interested in finding out about all this? Am I deeply concerned about this whole matter myself, questioning and looking as I go, as I sit, as I work with others? In my concern for peace, can there be clear awareness from moment to moment of the very activity of self that so permeates all human endeavor?

Anger

*When there is attention at the moment of
provocation, then listening takes the place of
habitual reaction. When images are clearly detected
and understood, provocation loses its power to
provoke.*

QUESTION. Toni, you often talk about objectively seeing and
accepting the way one is. And yet, I find a real dichotomy there.
I've been very angry and thoughtless and caused a lot of pain. I see
and feel it but still can't accept it within me.

TONI. I don't talk about accepting. Just seeing.

QUESTION. Isn't that accepting?

TONI. No. It has nothing to do with accepting.

QUESTION. You don't mention concrete ways of working on
these things. So I've got this idea of just accepting everything and
I feel a real resistance to doing that.

TONI. I understand that you don't like being angry and resist
accepting it. And yet anger comes up time and time again. Seeing
anger, listening to it very carefully without judgment, has nothing
to do with accepting it. Who is the accepter?

Is there an entity within anger or outside the anger to accept or
reject it? At the instant of anger, isn't there just an eruption of
physical and emotional reactions? Can that be faced directly as it
occurs? Not just reflecting upon it and analyzing it later when it is
all over, but seeing directly what is happening as it is happening,
without slipping into thoughts about accepting, condoning, con-
demning, controlling, or going beyond?

QUESTION. What is anger?

TONI. Somebody says or does something provocative, immedi-

This chapter contains an exchange that has been adapted from a question
period held in October 1983 at what was then the Genesee Valley Zen
Center.

ately triggering an inner state of psychological, physiological, neurological upheaval. Adrenaline is secreted, energy mounts, muscles tighten, the heart palpitates, the whole organism erupts in a physical and verbal explosion. There is an element of enjoyment in it too—the pleasure of physical release and of giving vent to pent-up feelings and emotions, either overtly, or in fantasy. Then, some time later, thinking starts up like this: "I'm angry and I shouldn't be," or "I am justified to be angry about this," or "This anger is not my True Self." Thinking about one's condition creates duality: It separates a thinking, judging "me" from the actual state of anger, and projects a future "me" without anger.

There is a strong feeling, a deeply rooted conviction that some kind of entity exists within, which is invaded by anger ("I am getting angry"), and which can take effective action against it ("I will control it, I shall overcome it"). This entity that feels separate from anger is thought: It is an idea, an image. It feels ever so real, but is it? Question it! It is an image, intricately connected with physcial sensations, emotions, feelings, will, resistance, and so on.

Can all this be seen and felt directly? It can, but nobody can do it for us.

Seeing is not thinking. Seeing is seeing—attending, listening without knowing.

If there is no clear awareness of how this human mind-and-body functions from moment to moment, division and conflict continue and multiply. Having an image of oneself and of what one should do or should not do creates duality and has nothing to do with undivided attention to what actually is taking place.

Attention comes from nowhere. It has no cause. It belongs to no one. When it functions effortlessly, there is no duality. Without attention, one lives in words, images, and memories of oneself and others, constantly in the grip of fear, anger, ambition, confusion.

QUESTION. There is just a feeling of the pain one has caused, and being tired of causing oneself and everyone else pain all the time. But there is also wanting to go beyond this and not be like that anymore. And yet I don't seem to be able to do anything about it. It's so frustrating. Around the house I'm always kicking the cat because I can't kick anyone else. Everyone else would kick me back. But, you know, every time I do it I die inside—and yet it remains a real routine.

TONI. Regretful thoughts about the past and wishful thoughts about what one would like to be in the future cannot and do not prevent anger from arising. Controlling and repressing anger do not do away with it either—it continues to smolder unconsciously (unattended to), ready to erupt again in distorted ways. Wanting to be rid of it, yet unable to attain a hoped-for state of calmness, results in new frustration and anger: One kicks the cat.

Is it at all possible to attend to anger directly as it is triggered in mind and body—observing carefully as it is actually unfolding, with energy gathering in intense inward looking and listening? It may be easier to attend while sitting down quietly, motionlessly— going to an empty room and listening to the inner turmoil without getting caught up in judgments for or against. But attention is not tied to sitting—it is not tied to anything and can occur any place at any time. It is instantaneous and irradiates thoughts, sensations, feelings, emotions, and physical reactions.

In clear, undivided attention, anger melts away—it loses its fuel and momentum. Its fuel and momentum are self-centered, dualistic thoughts, and the chain of reactions and counterreactions they trigger throughout the organism.

When there is attention at the moment of provocation, then listening takes the place of habitual reaction. When images are clearly detected and understood, provocation loses its power to provoke.

Can you discover this for yourself? Not just words, not just anger, but the root source of it all?

This is the very essence of this work of looking into oneself wholly, honestly, openly, gently, beyond all words, explanations, and resolutions.

Suffering

*It is for each one of us to see, understand, and end
the cause of conflict and sorrow in ourselves. The
understanding, the seeing, is the ending—no one is
doing it. When no one is there (doing the suffering
or trying to undo it) compassion arises on its own.*

Dear Toni,

My problem is pain (from serious injury, partial paralysis, and
repeated surgery) and time, waiting and wondering, when there is
so little I can control in my previously very tidy life. Much of the
time I can do nothing but wait . . . and feel commensurately
worthless. Most of all I am weary of being in pain and wonder
deeply if it has any meaning at all. When I was a Catholic (and a
nun for four years) we talked about "offering it up" and later in
Buddhism one talks of "transferring merit." Is there merit in
suffering?

Lately we have had many friends with tragedies in their lives,
including AIDS, drug addiction, paralysis, and so on. I find myself
wanting to lessen their pain by "offering up my own," but is this
possible, is it real? (If so I will complain no more.) The fact of
suffering is of course a "Noble Truth," but what does that really
mean? What does it mean in relation to compassion, to despair?

Dear ——,

You ask if there is merit in suffering. What would that merit
be?

Would it be the idea that through present pain something better,
more worthwhile, will be gained as a reward in the future?

Ideas and thoughts can be comforting and energizing to a

This chapter contains a letter to Toni from August 1986 and her response.

degree, but do they help one to be completely with the pain? Or do they distract from it? To be with pain completely, separation needs to end—and all thoughts about meaning, merit, and future states are distractions, aren't they? Can the mind remain alone (without the companionship of comforting thoughts), alert, flexible, undistorted, nongrasping, not escaping in the presence of intense physical pain? Can you find out? Is the pain still the same when there is no resistance whatsoever? Is the resistance the suffering?

You ask if you can offer up your pain to lessen the suffering of others. I stumbled over this question in preparing for confirmation in the Lutheran church in my teens. Jesus was said to have died for our sins, to have taken our guilt and suffering upon himself. But I felt no relief from mine, in spite of ardent attempts at "having faith." Looking at what was going on right around me, the crucifixion seemed to have made no impact at all on our sinning, which continued unabashedly through the horrors of war, persecution, holocaust.

What does it really mean to take on the sorrow of humankind? When there is no feeling of separation in oneself, no division into "me" and "the others," then there is also no division in pain and sorrow—it is one huge, deep, common, universal ocean of sorrow inundating all humankind. Can the pain and sorrow of this world, which is made up of the pain and sorrow of all uncountable human beings of all ages and times, be seen, felt, and understood deeply, clearly, without any sense of separateness? Without being crushed by it?

Physical pain may take its own time to abate or heal, but can mental, psychological pain end in this ending of resistance, conflict, and separation? No one can do this for anyone else. It is for each one of us to see, understand, and end the cause of conflict and sorrow in ourselves. The understanding, the seeing, is the ending— no one is doing it. When no one is there (doing the suffering or trying to undo it) compassion arises on its own.

Trust

*Can we face the seeming insecurity of constant
change and be open to the thoughts and feelings that
accompany this insecurity? Or do we cling to the
trust that everything will remain as we want it
to be?*

Recently several people have asked about the whole matter of
trust—what we mean by trust, what we mean when we say that
we trust someone. Also, what is the meaning of "trusting oneself"?

When we say and feel that we can trust someone, what do we
mean? We feel that we can trust a bookkeeper, don't we, when we
know from the past that he or she has been honest, conscientious,
and reliable. It means expecting past performance to continue into
the future without significant change. One assumes and predicts
that what has been happening will continue to happen.

Or, one meets someone for the first time and feels almost
immediately that he or she can be trusted. One's past remembered
experiences and impressions with someone who looks, speaks,
moves, and acts in a certain way make one feel that this person is
trustworthy.

Trusting that one's husband, wife, or lover will be faithful is
expecting the mutual commitment to continue without change:
he or she will not leave one for another. One assumes that what
has been remembered, felt, and promised in the past will also be
so in the future. So trusting means predicting with a sense of
security that things will continue in the way one expects and
wants them to.

One may of course be mistaken in one's knowledge about the
past—one may simply not have known about dishonesty in the
bookkeeper or in one's mate and be basing one's trust on false

---

The following chapter was written for the January 1989 *Springwater Center
Newsletter*.

ideas and assumptions. So trust is not necessarily based on facts. It is usually based on memory and on wishful thinking—the hope that what is known, or believed to have been, will continue to be so in the future.

This trust that is based on memory, belief, promise, and hope is easily but painfully betrayed when one comes in touch with actual facts, past or present. What one may have been so certain about in one's feelings toward a person may not have been true at all. Or, the person whom one thinks one knew and trusted has suddenly changed. Our moods, likes and dislikes, enthusiasms, and involvements do change.

So, can one see that one needs to look and listen directly, attentively, *right now,* without the automatic interference of illusions and wishful thinking? One may enjoy the security of trust based on past experiences and future predictions, but this cannot touch the reality of the immediacy and freshness of open awareness *now.*

Things within us and around us are changing all the time. Can we be aware of this without fear? Can we face the seeming insecurity of constant change and be open to the thoughts and feelings that accompany this insecurity? Or do we cling to the trust that everything will remain as we want it to be? Blind trust isn't open. It cannot see. Its security is illusory. It cannot possibly substitute for being awake and alert this very instant!

In saying this we're not implying that one should be distrustful or suspicious. Suspicion and distrust are based on memories and ideas, conscious as well as unconscious ones. One may have been disappointed and betrayed in one's expectations so many times and in such painful ways that there is great fear of being hurt all over again. Distrust is withdrawal out of fear of being hurt, isn't it? Can we look at that carefully as it comes up? Can one face and explore the fear of hurt and the desire to withdraw into a self-protective shell? What is one protecting? What gets hurt? Is one questioning all that?

People often say that they need an environment—therapeutic or otherwise—that they can trust, in order to open up to their deepest feelings and emotions. One would like to trust that in exploring and communicating honestly and deeply about oneself with others, one would not be exploited, ridiculed, humiliated, or otherwise hurt by the therapist, the teacher, or members of the group where such exploration takes place. Can we look at this more closely?

Looking into ourselves, coming face to face with deep feelings of anxiety, anger, hatred, violence, jealousy, envy, and guilt creates fear and pain, whether we do it in solitude or together with others. It creates fear and pain because we are finding out firsthand that we are not what we would like to be or have thought we were. We are *not* the ideal images that were ingrained into mind and body through parents, educators, religious teachers, and other models. We are not ideal personages, no matter how much we may be attached to and identified with ideal images about ourselves.

We all are of the same common stock of conditioned reactions and emotions, and we all share the same fear and guilt about not being what we feel we ought to be. At one time we may feel superior to others, yet at another moment feel utterly inferior to everyone else. We want to feel powerful and important and at the same time are afraid of weakness and humiliation. We are afraid of being at fault and getting blamed, and would rather find fault elsewhere and blame others. Somewhere we all feel an insatiable need for being loved unconditionally, but we have great difficulty in finding this love within ourselves. In one form or another and to one degree or another all this is true for every one of us. Can one investigate this for oneself, looking quietly, patiently?

If we look closely, honestly, we find that we are not unique. Discovering the truth about ourselves is discovering the truth about "others." Once we realize how utterly similar we are to each other in our needs, reactions, and emotions, we will not be so afraid of getting hurt by "others." Hurt in ourselves and hurt in "others" is the same hurt. Instead of evading and avoiding hurt, can it be felt thoroughly, deeply, and be understood compassionately through direct insight? Can we work alone and together in this way?

You may ask: If two people come together with a deep sense of friendship and openness for each other, with goodwill and shared interest in something—doesn't that mean they *trust* each other?

Let us look again: When there is this coming together in friendship and shared interest, meeting each other unconditionally, we may *describe* this as "trust," but there is no need to create an *idea* of "trust" and hang on to that.

Everything is there when we meet unconditionally, isn't it?

Everything is there, as it is, without protective shells, without escape or fear. This moment is alive and whole. The moment I begin to defend and protect myself and withdraw, what becomes of trust? Can one see? "Trusting" is slipping again into imagination and hope for security, away from the aliveness of simply being there with what is, without any sense of separateness.

If this is clearly understood, then what does it mean to trust oneself? Sometimes people say that one cannot trust another as long as one doesn't trust oneself. But what is the self that one wishes to trust? Can one ask this question and freely observe the endless manifestations of self—fear, suffering, loneliness, wanting, anger, hatred, lack of love, and the insatiable demand for security? That is the self—what is there to be trusted?

As long as the sense of self dominates and distorts perception and reaction it precludes direct awareness. There is the demand for trust, but at the same time, the utter inability to trust. The need for and the inability to trust both spring out of the isolation of self.

Only when the self abates in direct insight may love come into being on its own. Love has no needs, no fears, no trust nor distrust. It is not apart. It is not something I do. In love there is neither "you" nor "me."

Abortion

If one examines all of one's motives carefully and honestly one may find that every one of them is self-centered, whether it is to keep the baby or to have an abortion. Can this fact be faced directly, nonjudgmentally? Can self-centeredness be fully aired in awareness without choice?

Dear Toni,

I am questioning my feelings, ideas, images, regarding abortion, since there will be an abortion service at the center I work in.

My strong Catholic background has given my mind numerous ideas and images to deal with. Fear of "going to hell" for working with abortion has come up.

Is the fetus really in pain?

I suppose a no or yes answer may not be correct at all.

Oftentimes the woman who needs and wants the abortion has pain and anguish to deal with—especially if she were told she had to carry to term or couldn't have an abortion.

I know I need to work through these fears and images. Do you have any suggestions?

Dear _____,

You ask: "Is the fetus really in pain?"

Why does one ask this question? Does it arise from one's anxiety and guilt about causing pain to someone else? And not wanting to feel that anguish?

Why does one think of the fetus as something separate? Isn't it an integral part of the total being of the mother, who is not separate from all human beings?

This chapter contains edited excerpts from a letter to Toni from April 1986 and her response.

If the mother suffers pain—physical or mental—doesn't that affect her whole being, which includes the fetus in her womb? And if there is dysfunction or trauma in the fetus, doesn't that affect the mother's organism and in turn everyone related to her and through her?

Why do we consider anything separately?

We human beings are thoroughly conditioned and trained to think in separate compartments, focusing on one thing to the exclusion of everything else. We may have passionate ideas about the right of the fetus to continue its life inside and outside the womb, and yet completely ignore the fact that we may indoctrinate our children or allow them to be indoctrinated to kill and be killed for the sake of patriotic, ideological, or religious causes.

Our concern for human beings, born or not yet born, is largely motivated by our inherited and accumulated ideas about the meaning and purpose of life. We take these ideas as absolute and yet they vary widely from one era to the next and from one culture to another.

In many present-day poverty-stricken countries the custom still prevails that children will take care of aging parents. To have many children constitutes the only social security. Abortion of future children would be an absurdity.

In present-day China the government is trying to curb overpopulation by limiting each family to one child only. Having more than one child is punishable. Abortion is one of the ways of cutting down population.

In Hitler's Germany even single women were encouraged to have babies. "Give the Fuehrer a child!" was the slogan. There had to be ever-increasing supplies of human beings to man the conquering marches into other countries and to take care of their continued occupation.

Many religious organizations condemn abortion. Is it because of ideas about the God-given sacredness of life and the fear of trespassing against God's will? Are there also political motives involved?

In this country abortion has become a powerful political issue. As such it can be used to gain power solely for the sake of gaining power. Identification with a political issue easily serves the fanaticism to win. Violence in one form or another ensues inevitably.

Abortion is labeled "murder." Abortion clinics have been bombed and life threats made against people involved in performing abortion. In any conflict or struggle, be it religious or political, there cannot possibly be love. Love is killed when we fight over the right to live.

Do we realize how our deep attachments to ideas and beliefs affect our relationships, causing conflicts and contradictions within ourselves and with each other? How can there possibly be loving care for another human being as long as the mind is functioning in inherited or newly adopted thinking grooves that one is not even aware of? Can all our beliefs and ideas be openly questioned and brought to light without fear?

So, in meeting and working together with pregnant women who are in anguish about whether to abort or to keep the baby— can you question together our ideas and beliefs with their connected threats of punishment and promises of reward? Can prejudices that are discovered be put aside so that one can begin to think factually and spaciously about what is involved in having a baby or in having an abortion?

In discussing and looking together, is one obsessed with finding a solution to the problem? This is how we usually deal with all our problems. We try to figure them out by thinking back and forth, going over the same stuff again: whether the fetus is conscious life, whether it feels pain, whether one will end up in hell, whether the guilt or grief of loss will be too much.

This frantic searching for an answer is the franticness of the self that is desperately trying to find the best solution for itself. If one examines all of one's motives carefully and honestly one may find that every one of them is self-centered, whether it is to keep the baby or to have an abortion. Can this fact be faced directly, nonjudgmentally? Can self-centeredness be fully aired in awareness without choice?

Is it humanly possible to look at a problem without the interference of the self? Can one look without ingrained beliefs, without fearing for oneself or desiring anything for oneself? Can one start right now?

Giving birth to a child—doesn't it involve enormous responsibility to take good care of it, to bring it up healthily and sanely without unconsciously imposing upon this young life all the confusions, illusions, and violence manifesting in oneself? Is there the time, the patience, and the love to grow up together, question- ing, looking, and acting freely, regardless of punishments and rewards? Would one give one's whole life to that?

In talking with someone, does one realize how little we can actually know? How uncertain we are? How our yearning for a secure self gets frustrated and foiled time and time again?

Can all the fears, pains, and doubts that accompany this shared work be deeply felt and seen together without giving way to any escapes?

Fear of Death

What is this fear of personal death that torments us?
Can we allow it to unfold and reveal itself in the
stillness of questioning-attending, no matter how
strong the urge to escape?

Dear Toni,

I am writing because I have recently come in touch with a great deal of fear. After I attended a workshop dealing with the psychological problems of the nuclear age, the television film *The Day After* was shown. I helped organize a community gathering in my neighborhood to share our feelings that came up about the film. All these horrible military and political events suddenly became real for me. As if a curtain went up, I have suddenly seen how terribly dangerous this world is! I have been gripped by an almost paralyzing fear. Work is the only thing that really takes my mind off it. I have been sitting and this helps, but even there I encounter such terrible panic. I feel a much stronger need to know who I am, believing that if I find out, I won't be so afraid to die.

I find myself casting about for escape routes, even thinking, "This is only happening to force me to be serious about my Zen work! They *can't* mean it." I feel frozen, and then great pain when I let some of the beauty of life in. I'd like the fear to go away, and I'm afraid to let it go, afraid I will go back to sleep.

Partly I realize that I might die sooner than expected. I know this has to do with my fear of personal death. (This is different from the panic I feel in recalling scenes of bombs going off.) It is simply that I don't want to stop living yet!

I don't know what I am asking for here—certainly not for you to tell me everything will be all right. I have been listening to some of your tapes, and I would appreciate a letter.

This chapter contains a letter to Toni from April 1984 and her response.

Dear _____,

We do get in touch with a great deal of fear: paralyzing fear and panic at the thought of nuclear bombs going off, and a different kind of fear of personal death. We don't like these fears and want them to go away. Yet we are afraid that if they go away, we will go back to sleep. Fear may impel us to sit and question more intensely, and we hope that this may be a way out.

Our habitual reaction to fear is to try to get rid of it. Instead of that, can one face it directly, wholly, and come upon its root cause? Only in facing it immediately, understanding it thoroughly, realizing one *is* fear, does it lose its overwhelming power over our life.

Can there be utter stillness in the full presence of fear, attending silently, motionlessly, as it arises and unravels? Being utterly still implies not wanting any rewarding results to come out of this stillness—simply attending to what is actually happening, without blockage, judgment, or expectation of better states to come. Can one do this?

What is fear? Can we watch the total process?

The instant we see something that threatens our survival, strong physiological responses take place throughout the organism: energy rises, the heartbeat accelerates, the stomach closes up, intestines churn, muscles flex, senses narrow down. Our inherited animal instincts, programmed in the brain, prepare the body to flee, to attack, or to freeze.

If a real physical danger is present and we can actually take off and run, the mobilized energy serves its purpose; the demand for instant action is fulfilled. Running away from a falling tree is an appropriate response. Seeing and running are one complete action.

However, what frightens us most of the time is not immediate danger, but worry about our physical and psychological existence: *thoughts* about what *may* happen to us in the *future*. These thoughts stem from the remembrance of past painful or terrifying experiences, something that we either have experienced ourselves or recollect from hearsay—books, news reports, movies, and so forth.

Thoughts about past and future dangers trigger the same physical fear reactions that real present dangers do, but we don't carry out what we are physically programmed to do: We don't get up and run. We just continue thinking, imagining, and emoting: "What is going to happen to me? What will it be like? It will be disastrous! What am I going to do? Am I going to die?" With each new thought and image more physical symptoms appear that in turn create additional mental reactions: "I don't like this anxiety. It's becoming unbearable. I want it to stop. How can I get out of this?" Verbalizing about one's condition itself creates distress. Wanting to get rid of distress creates conflict and separation, which in turn creates more tension and distress.

Do you see the avalanching effects of thought throughout this body-mind? Do you see and feel it directly as it is actually happening? Or do you try to get away from it?

Getting absorbed in work, in social or political movements, in entertainment, sports, drink, sex, or religious pursuits temporarily may take the mind off frightening thoughts and physical disturbance, but cannot bring inner freedom. Escapes do not terminate fear. They temporarily drive it underground. Sooner or later thoughts return to the threat—the bombs or whatever—fear resurfaces, the whole process starts going again.

Thinking about a danger from which there is no escape at all—like a global nuclear holocaust—may not even allow any imaginary refuge to run to. Although all our inherited inner systems are GO!, the mobilized energy can't be discharged. Only confused thinking continues, resulting in states of panic or paralysis.

Can we see that thoughts about the past, present, and future are the cause of fear? Can we see that "past," "present," and "future" are thoughts themselves?

Without memories of myself in the past, and projections of myself into the future, there is no fear! My "self" is a thought too—actually a collection of many different ideas, identifications, and images (with their connected emotions, motivations, and goals) accumulated throughout the past. We fear and tremble for these images—afraid that the picture story of our personal life may come to an untimely, unhappy ending. Look at it, question it—see it for yourself. Without memories of past events and anticipations of future dangers is there fear? There is only what is *actually* going on right this instant, as it is. This may be immediate danger and instantaneous action, but there is no problem in this.

What is this fear of personal death that torments us? Can we allow it to unfold and reveal itself in the stillness of questioning-attending, no matter how strong the urge to escape?

What is personal death?

Asking this question and pausing to look inward—isn't personal death a concept? Isn't there a thought-and-picture series going on in the brain? These scenes of personal ending take place solely in the imagination, and yet they trigger great mental and physical distress—thinking of one's cherished attachments and their sudden, irreversible termination.

Similarly, if there is "pain when I let some of the beauty of life in"—isn't this pain the result of thinking, "I won't be here any longer to enjoy this beauty?" Or, "*No one* will be around and no beauty left to be enjoyed if there is total nuclear devastation."

Apart from the horrendous tragedy of human warfare—why is there this fear of "me" not continuing? Is it because I don't realize that all my fear and trembling is for an image? Because I really believe that this image is myself?

In the midst of this vast, unfathomable, ever-changing, dying, and renewing flow of life, the human brain is ceaselessly engaged in trying to fix for itself a state of permanency and certainty. Having the capacity to think and form pictures of ourselves, to remember them and become deeply attached to them, we take this world of pictures and ideas for real. We thoroughly believe in the reality of the picture story of our personal life. We are totally identified with it and want it to go on forever. The idea of "forever" is itself an invention of the human brain. Forever is a dream.

Questioning beyond all thoughts, images, memories, and beliefs, questioning profoundly into the utter darkness of not-knowing, the realization may suddenly dawn that one is nothing at all—nothing—that all one has been holding on to are pictures and dreams. Being nothing is being everything. It is wholeness. Compassion. It is the ending of separation, fear, and sorrow.

Is there pain when no one is there to hold on?

There is beauty when there is no "me."

Living Together

*Can we human beings share life on earth together
without trying to own each other or trying to get rid
of each other?*

We human beings want to live in happiness, security, and love, but
even though this is our constant endeavor, we don't really know
what will bring it about.

We think, we dream, and we talk about happiness and security.
We also talk and dream about love—imagine it, long for it, pray
for it, promise it to each other, and pursue it strenuously. But
genuine happiness, security, and love aren't products of anything.
They cannot be made intentionally. They cannot be possessed.
And if they are dreams and ideas they are not genuine. They come
uninvited when the mind is still and open, not engaged in the
conflicting movements of self-centeredness. They arise unexpect-
edly when the mind is not in want or fear and therefore not in
pursuit of anything.

One wonders, "Why are we unhappy, insecure, and without
love?"

Can we begin to question and attend carefully, impartially, in
our moment-to-moment living together at home, at work, or
wherever we may be? Can there be the newness of questioning,
discovering, understanding, and caring about one another?

Discovering, understanding, and caring do not arise in a mind
that is enclosed in fixed ideas about itself and others. In living
together, can there be openness and genuine interest in whatever
may be coming up in both you and me at *this* moment—be it
desire and longing, prejudice and fear, tenderness or tension, anger
or pleasure, misunderstanding, loneliness, rejection, blockage, a
feeling of isolation, or whatever?

This chapter was written for the October 1988 *Springwater Center Newsletter.*

Can there be a deepening interest in directly exploring what moves and compels all of us consciously and unconsciously? Can we be directly aware of what is going on inside us and between us—not only superficially but deeply?

Is it possible to be in ever fresh and intimate touch with all the various complex thoughts and emotions in ourselves and the "other," not labeling anything as either bad or good? No labeling! Are we aware how instantaneously judgment comes up? Can this be seen without condemnation or acceptance?

Two people living together—can we meet each other afresh each new day, not clinging to the memory of what happened yesterday, in years gone by, or just a moment ago?

Every instant of life is new and fresh. Can we actually perceive the truth of this and live that way, or are we forever stuck with the endless succession of pleasant and painful memories? Clearly this baggage can drop! Can it happen this instant, or will one continue to nurse memories over and over?

Can we be with each other without the heavy influence of old images, even though we have collected images of ourselves and each other over a whole lifetime? Are we aware how these images color and distort our perceptions of each other? How they actually prevent us from perceiving anything accurately this moment? If we clearly understand this, can we carefully—caringly—look again as though for the very first time?

Is it possible to look at each other and listen to each other in an entirely new way—not habitually driven to correct or change each other according to our likes and dislikes? Can we newly discover what is actually going on this instant and respond from clarity rather than from ideas?

There are so many questions . . . Is one just reading them casually, hastily, or can one actually pause quietly to wonder and look at all this profoundly?

This universe is infinite space. Can there be space to let be what happens to be this instant, without an immediate reaction? Just the stillness of awareness without immediately knowing and finding fault? As soon as the fault-finding mechanism sets into motion, anger, resentment, and guilt enclose and becloud the mind and nothing can be seen truthfully.

What does it mean to see each other exactly as we are? Past

memories about ourselves and each other are *not* what we are right now. Memory is an incomplete and inaccurate recording of the past. Now is something entirely different. Quietly looking and listening *now* is not memory. It is an entirely different mode of mind. It is a cleansing of perception.

The other day the little stream that runs near the center was gushing noisily downhill with lots of muddy water hiding its depth. Today it is flowing quietly, clearly, exposing sheets of brightly shimmering green bedrock.

Can we see things just as they are right now? Without wanting them to be otherwise? Without comparing them favorably or unfavorably? Without wanting them to stay this way forever? Without clinging and depending? Without wanting to own and possess?

Can we human beings share life on earth together without trying to own each other or trying to get rid of each other? The idea of possessing each other gives an illusory sense of security. Along with it inevitably goes the fear of losing what we have become accustomed and attached to.

With the loss of another—real or imagined—comes the pain of grieving, of feeling forsaken, abandoned, lost, and sorry for oneself. With the idea of losing someone to somebody else comes the agony of jealousy, anger, hate, and violence. One can verify all this thoroughly by oneself. We may cling to each other for fear of losing each other, but possessing someone has nothing to do with love. Possessions cause pride as well as fear, dependency, and sorrow. Love knows no fear and no dependency. It has no possessions and no attachments. Love is without sorrow.

As one watches the trees in the evening sky, their trunks and branches aglow with the golden light of the setting sun, the gentle sounds of peepers, insects, and birds, a distant plane streaking across the sky, the fragrance of the evening air and the rustling leaves alive with movement, everything all at once swaying, humming, and glistening in the breeze, the clouds moving swiftly, with their constantly changing shapes and colors disappearing and appearing out of nowhere . . . there is nothing separate and nothing obstructing anything else in this total movement of aliveness. There is space for everything happening freely, nothing lording it over anything else, yet everything inseparably linked with everything else. Everything *is* everything else!

This whole everything, which is no separate things, never remains the same from one instant to the next, and yet each moment is totally sufficient, whole, and without conflict.

We are not separate from all this! There is no separate movement of "me" and "mine" except in thought-feeling and memory.

Deeply realizing the beauty of this is love and joy and the ending of insecurity.